A LITTLE COUNTRY

JULIA USMAN

A LITTLE COUNTRY

This is a non-fiction book based on the personal reflections and experiences of the author. The names of people have been changed to protect their privacy; village and town names remain unaltered.

First published in hardback format by Coverstory books, 2022

ISBN 978-1-7397660-8-5

Copyright © Julia Usman 2022

The right of Julia Usman to be identified as the author of this work has been asserted by them in accordance with the Copyright, Designs and Patents Act 1988.

Cover image © Helen Alice Johnson
[www.helenalicejohnsonartist.com].

All rights reserved.

No part of this publication may be reproduced, circulated, stored in a system from which it can be retrieved, or transmitted in any form without the prior permission in writing of the publisher.

www.coverstorybooks.com

For my children and grandchildren

Contents

FOREWORD 5

✻

HEFTED 7
MAPPING 11
ROOTS 21
PLACE 27
SEASONS 39
BIRTH AND DEATH 63
GROWING UP 75
VOICE 83
TRACKS 97
BONES 107
LOSS 115
WALLS 121
COMMUNITY 125
CUSTOMS 145
TIME 151
FAREWELL 155
LEGACY 161

✻

Acknowledgements 165
Bibliography 167

Swaledale in Yorkshire is a little country in itself.[1]

'...once, on this earth, once, on this familiar spot of ground, walked other men and women, as actual as we are today, thinking their own thoughts, swayed by their own passions, but now all gone, one generation vanishing into another, gone as utterly as we ourselves shall shortly be gone, like ghosts at cockcrow...'[2]

'Yet there are places and times on this Earth when the ground grows thin, and the dead arise of themselves...They must be spoken with, if we are to remain honest.'[3]

---

[1] Pontefract, Ella & Hartley, Marie, 1934, *Swaledale*, London: J.M, Dent & Sons Ltd.
[2] Trevelyan, G.M., *Autobiography of a Historian*, 1949.
[3] Greig, Andrew, 2010, *At The Loch Of The Green Corrie*, London: Quercus Editions Ltd.

FOREWORD

I inhabit the lore I have inherited. The daughter of farming parents, I am propagated by ancestors from the soils of northern England. My Yorkshire upbringing was nurtured in a tight-knit rural community of small farms rooted in Methodism and centuries of customs: steady lives, accepting, conservative, cyclical.

As time and distance from the community in which I was brought up increases, the more these early rural influences accompany me on my journey through life, down tracks that bring into focus the threads that stitch my identity. None more so than the people and experiences that walk alongside me from childhood. In these vanishing clusters of small mixed farms, there is a story to carry into the future, to tell before a way of life completely disappears from living memory.

This is a story of landscape and community, a way of life descended from Anglo-Saxon and Viking farmers. It is a story that could belong to anyone who has lived their early years growing up on a modest dairy farm in the 1960s and 70s. It is about static lives, and about movement, about change, and about understanding how the past walks through us, mapping our present and future.

I am nurtured by layers of limestone; the quiet voices that hide in the fells and dales of northern England. But distant places also teach about home and the nuances that influence and shape. No matter where I choose to stay awhile, I am flux, straying in and out of memories.

Whilst the present is a winding road that has taken me through the Middle East and back into Swaledale, I carry my early years spent in a little country. A little country that no longer exists in the form it once did; except, that is, in every fibre of me.

I walk the old bridleways, the veins of the dales, their paths are journeys that lead me into other lands, and in quiet moments, take me back to my heart.

HEFTED
'the past is there like a scent'[4]

I perch on the back doorstep of our farmhouse porch with a black and white rough-haired border collie. It is her first summer with us. We have an affinity, both having recently reached our fifth birthdays. Together we absorb our world as we sit side-by-side. I have just started school and have decided that one week is quite enough to learn all the teacher has to offer and will not be returning after the weekend. This suggestion has received a firm rebuttal from my mother, leaving me confused. Lassie's instinctive empathy provides solace. It is curious how many lessons we learn from animals.

Father has recently agreed to give Lassie a home. Since being a pup, she has lived with the Clarkson family in a neighbouring village, but their absence during working hours has led her into the habit of chewing her way through lonely days. Re-homed on our farm, she seems to settle quickly into her new life. Here, her instinct to herd cows and sheep is put to full use. She appears to adapt willingly, roaming the farmstead by day, happy to curl up in her warm kennel at night.

One day she vanishes.

'She can't have gone far.'

My father consoles me and my siblings as we search barns and byres with increasing concern.

'She might be next door, she likes ol' Roy.'

Roy was a craggy tan collie; he greets us with a wagging tail as we race into the farmyard bumping straight into our neighbour, Joseph. Joseph, in our youthful opinion, is incredibly old, but a combination of an easy smile and a small, wiry stature gives him a sprite-like air that is endearing. Clean-shaven, he possesses an unusually neat appearance for farmers of our acquaintance, with his grandad-collar shirt buttoned up to the chin, waistcoat and tweed jacket, all topped with the requisite flat cap. Never without the appendage of a polished, wooden pipe protruding from the side of his mouth, a long draw of breath and a slow puff of smoke produced solutions to many problems.

'Nay...nivver seen her. But best take a look.'

---

[4] James Sheard, *Scent*.

We gallop through the warren of stone buildings, along dim and dusky passages, calling her name.

Later, when Lassie has missed her tea, my father confesses:

'I'm beginnin' to worry.'

Eventually, as darkness descends over our search, my mother calls out from the kitchen window.

'I've had Mr Clarkson on the phone. Would you believe it. He's just got home and she's sat on his doorstep.'

'What! How's she got there?'

'He's going to pop her back to us now.'

But only days after Mr Clarkson returns her, Lassie once more makes her way over the three miles distance between the farm and her old home.

'Oh…why doesn't she like it here?' we moan as we mooch around our mother's ankles.

'It's not that she doesn't like it with us, it's just that she's lived with the Clarkson's since she was a pup. It's that invisible thread that pulls her back.'

'What invisible thread? Why can't we see it?'

'Because it comes from inside her.'

This was a very baffling comment.

The more Lassie made her way back to her original home, both parents began to match our bewilderment; when she was with us, she appeared to enjoy herself. She shadowed my father as he went about his daily foddering, was happy to greet us when we returned from school, and soon learned from experience she needed to give the farm cats the respect they demanded. The rest of her day was spent watching the comings and goings, helping bring the cows in for milking, or sitting by our back door waiting for titbits.

Her only flash of inexplicable character came when one particular postman, Davey, was on duty. From his first visit after her arrival, she pounced at his vehicle door, reaching up, barking and baring her teeth. At a nervous five feet tall, there was nothing that could persuade Davey to get out of his van and face up to Lassie, and the initial impression he made on her never mellowed. She knew as soon as the red mail van drove into the yard if he was at the wheel; all the other postmen were made welcome with a wagging tail.

Despite her apparent enjoyment in scaring Davey, this new source of entertainment did not distract Lassie from thoughts of her former home, and she continued to abandon the farm when no one was keeping an eye on her.

'How does she know which way to go?'

'We're not allowed on the road and we're human!'

'She's only a dog so why is she so clever?'

We could not fathom out how Lassie managed to negotiate traffic and junctions, frightened she would be knocked down.

'I think she follows her nose,' our mother reflected.

'Nose? But her nose is joined on to her. It doesn't have legs.'

'No, silly. She can smell home on the wind.'

'What!'

'Try it for yourself next time and see.'

'Huh!'

Sometimes parents said the stupidest things, unless, of course, they were thinking of the familiar whiff of the muck heap as it mingled with every bit of breeze that blew through our yard, summer and winter alike.

Eventually after a great deal of cupboard love and time spent with her, Lassie settled down to life with us; but not before teaching me home is not where you want to be, it is where you must be.

Lassie enjoying retirement in the garden whilst tolerating the youthfulness of kittens; animals living side by side.

My father joined an organisation called 'British Boys for British Farms'[5] when he left school, aged fifteen, in Newcastle upon Tyne. He hailed from a Northumberland farming background and spent most of his young life with his grandparents in the rural backdrop of Stamfordham, forging lifelong connections with the people and surrounding countryside. He was born in the village where his grandparents and great-grandparents had lived, and uncles and great-uncles still farmed, and where his father was the local butcher, until his premature death at the age of thirty-five.

After finishing his training at Mappleton[6] on the East Yorkshire coast, he was placed on a farm at Catterick in the North Riding of Yorkshire with Mr and Mrs Atkinson; a childless couple who were now nearing retirement age and in need of help. Ted Atkinson was a veteran of the First World War, and their farm, Prospect Farm, was part of a County Council initiative that had been set up to give returning soldiers interested in working on the land a chance to start up and make a living in agriculture.

Mr Atkinson was a cow man and began to teach my father about blood lines. The Atkinson's showed their cattle at local agricultural events and so my father was swiftly cultivated into the art of judging good stock and assessing the breeding programmes that were put in place to enhance the milking herd. He joined the local football team and Young Farmer's Club, soon becoming initiated into the ways of Yorkshire men.

But he was forged from the land west of Newcastle, and like a homing pigeon, made his way sixty miles north whenever he had time off from work. Before he had enough money saved to buy a car, this meant cycling up the Great North Road, now the A1(M), along a route that has been used by travellers for over ten thousand years.[7]

The umbilical was never severed. My father kept his formative accent in the sixty-five years he lived in Yorkshire. His genes were mapped; his internal compass, like that of our dog, resolutely pointing to his earliest home.

---

[5] A YMCA training scheme (1932-1968) was set up to help young boys, many from urban backgrounds, who were interested in agriculture. They gained skills that led to permanent work on the land, and for some, to their own farms.

[6] Mappleton camp was requisitioned by the army in World War II from the YMCA who had used it as a holiday camp pre-war. Later, before it finally closed in the 1960s, it was used to house refugees.

[7] The A1 is the longest numbered road in the UK, stretching 410 miles between London and Scotland. Originally thought to have been built by the Romans, it follows Ermine Street between London and York, then Dere Street from York to Edinburgh. Recent archaeological evidence proves the route is much older. Remains of Neolithic, Mesolithic and Iron age settlements have been discovered near Catterick when digging before the upgrades made in the second decade of the 21st century.

MAPPING
'affirmed and scattered by landscape'[8]

I am given an atlas for Christmas when I am nine years old. My father owns a well-turned Bartholomew road-atlas of Great Britain. Bartholomew maps are an adventure. The colours of burnt orange, deep sandalwoods and cobalt are my first poems.

Deep colours signify the highest points of land on a map. Trace a finger over the contours of the Yorkshire Dales and you will hear the curlew, smell the clouds that have travelled the Atlantic to rise over the Pennines, exhausted of rain. Here, the westerly weather continues to chisel and sculpt. Let your thoughts stay for a while amongst the margins of the fields, stroll ancient lanes, touch parish boundary stones, roam over flag, grits and plate.[9] Taste the pith that binds you to this earth.

Swaledale maps into the DNA of all who hail from this northern-most part of Yorkshire; each contour of land a differing shade of Brigante, Roman, Anglo Saxon, Viking, Norman. Scratch the surface of the soil and stir the flesh; nature, culture and history are one.

§

When the first farmers settled in Swaledale, it was covered in forests of pine, larch and beech, prowled by wolves and scoured by boar. During the 1st century A.D., the ancient woodlands began to be cleared for agricultural use by farmer-warrior Anglo Saxons. Later, seafaring invaders, the Vikings, brought with them their communal ways of farming, living in clusters, sharing common land and grazing rights. They integrated well, marrying into the local population. Then in the 11th century the Norman Kings claimed their rights to the English throne and, with their Breton and Flemish soldiers, settled around *Richemont*,[10] introducing forms of enclosure for more efficient farming methods. But the dales remained sparsely populated with only a small number of villages

---

[8] Robert Macfarlane writing of Edward Thomas in *The Old Ways: A Journey on Foot*.
[9] Swaledale was formed in the Carboniferous Period and is part of Yoredale series of rock. Local miners named the three main rock formations found in the dale - limestone/flag, sandstone/grits or gritstone and shale/plate. However, some of the sandstone found in Swaledale is less 'grit', or coarse, than sandstones elsewhere. Both lead and coal were mined in the past.
[10] Richmond, 'rich mountain/hill'. This is the original place of this name; there are 56 Richmond's around the world.

until the mining boom of the 18th century that left its scars on the skin of the land we see today.[11]

This remains a landscape populated by the spirits of those who once dwelled within it. Look deeper into time and it will yield ancient voices. Even now they are reaching out, enabling the twenty-first century traveller to touch their stories, embrace what they have left behind in the forms of myths and superstitions, or in physical markers embedded onto and in the earth, such as stone circles and flints. Search the faces of families who have lived and worked, shaped and re-shaped these uplands century after century, note the structure of their foreheads, their cheekbones, the colour of their hair.

Sometime in the 8th or 9th century, *Gunnarr*, a Norse chief, settled in a clearing, now the village of Gunnerside. His legacy remains firmly sewn into the area. His language still influences the vernacular despite the centuries that have passed. My family name illustrates the mixed influences of those who came to dominate the area known as Northumbria in the Dark Ages:[12] Richardson, with origins in Anglo Saxon, ric meaning power; hard meaning brave, son as we know it, derived from the old Norse manner of attributing patriarchal lineage.

From my kingdom of ice, I rise with your water. I am the fells, the dales, my warrior body this backbone of land. I leave you my hand that fought against a savage death, leave you my voice spliced tongue into tongue, leave you my veins blood of your blood, leave you my name to be the name of your sons, the bones of your fathers are my bones. I leave you my words to keep on your lips, my epitaph is your song, your home, your river. I leave you my gods to watch over your skies. I am your stars, your dust.

§

We lived on a rise of land almost central to the east and west coasts of Northern England and were brought up dipping our toes into both the North and the Irish Seas at Saltburn and Morecambe, respectively.

From our modest hill, the farm had an aspect that was open and far reaching. The North York Moors silhouetted against a distinct horizon, visible over thirty miles across the vale, and when clouds dispersed, we glimpsed the puffing

---

[11] Mining in the area can be traced back to the Romans. Evidence of 18th and 19th century mining can be seen at sights such as Grinton Moor and Gunnerside Gill in Swaledale.
[12] Northumbria included, at the height of the kingdom's power, land from the Firth of Forth in Scotland to the Humber estuary in Yorkshire.

cigarette chimneys of ICI on Teesside coughing a constant murky soot into the atmosphere.

The Great North Road, in the days of stagecoaches, ran through the centre of Catterick. Here, old hostelries remain in evidence today. During the 1950s the road was upgraded to become the A1 dual carriageway, now the A1(M), bypassing the village to weave in and out of the barley and wheat fields that still lie half a mile to the east of the land we farmed. A functional concrete flyover bridged the A1 on the road that wandered down to the primary school, bank, grocer, butcher, post office, hairdresser, and until the early 1970s, a toy shop.

At Catterick Bridge, the railway station welcomed my father's sister from Newcastle once a year. The white painted signal box was permanently staffed; the gates heaved opened at the level crossing as trains passed through and onwards to the neighbouring stations of Scorton to the east and Richmond to the west. The line was closed as part of the Beeching cuts in 1969. Now the platform has made way for a caravan and camping retail outlet where the discourse of journeys and discovery continues.

Close by, a racecourse gallops alongside the A1.[13] The main grandstand was the standout feature easily spotted from our kitchen window. On race days, with the wind in the right direction, the course commentary drifted across fields and into our yard in a purr of incoherent notes like a radio station not quite tuned in. Excitement and cheering from the winning post rubbed alongside the solitude of our little community.

From the back of the house at night, out across the fields and over the racetrack, starlit Scotch Corner marked the crossroads between the north-south A1, and the east-west A66 which carried traffic up over Bowes Moor and the Pennines towards the west, then northwards into a land called Scotland that we knew only by name as we had never visited. This major junction beamed in a constellation of red and orange, guiding our eyes northwards. A trig point from our stationary hilltop, but a beacon for thousands on the move.

Because of my father's Northumbrian roots, the north was a magnet. Travelling the old Roman road, Dere Street[14] for much of the way, the drive was straight and uncomplicated but we were always impatient to arrive:

'Are we there yet?'

---

[13] One of 17 out of 60 courses in the UK that provide for both flat and jump meetings.
[14] Dere Street formed part of our straight route up into Northumberland from Catterick before we turned off it close to Corbridge and headed the last few miles firstly on the military road, then on windy rural lanes to Stamfordham. (The military road was not Roman but built in 1740s to enable troops to travel quickly because of the Jacobite threat from across the Scottish border).

'Nearly, just seven horizons.'

My father measured journeys in horizons.

'Uhhh.'

He might as well have said round Cape Horn and up to Morocco; the distance was indefinable from the seat in the back of our Austin Maxi.

Southern destinations were few and far between. Once we had a holiday in North Wales, but most years the furthest south we ventured would be in July to the Great Yorkshire Show at Harrogate, thirty-five miles away.[15]

Prospect Farm stood at the end of a potholed track two fields back from Tunstall Road. Here, turning east at the lane end, we freewheeled downhill onto a wide village green,[16] Catterick, where the Romans built a fortification, named Cataractonium[17], and St Paulinus[18] is said to have baptised ten thousand believers on one day in the River Swale in the 7th century. In the early twentieth century, one of the first WW1 RAF airfields[19] came to nestle into the land that lies on the southern fringes of the settlement.

Turn west out of the farm lane and after about two miles the linear village of Tunstall slumbered, hardly waking to notice as we passed through. Once beyond the village the battle with the prevailing wind began. After a climb through rolling pastures for five miles or so, an imaginary edge-land was crossed merging moorlands and errant clouds, realigning us with ice-forged dales.

Often on summer Sunday afternoons our parents loaded us into the car and drove us into these upland folds. Both heather moors and riverbanks seduced us in equal measures, alongside the company of dragonflies, rabbits, red admiral butterflies, a sober heron, and if we were lucky, a kingfisher flashing neon and bringing gasps of:

'Did you see that blue lightening?'

---

[15] Founded in 1837 it was known as the Yorkshire Agricultural Society Show and renamed the Great Yorkshire Show early in the twentieth century. It is now the largest agricultural show in England.

[16] The road has since been altered to accommodate the widening of the A1(M).

[17] Bronze and Iron Age evidence has been found in the area; Romans are thought to have arrived around AD70.

[18] The Swale was known as the 'Jordan of England' at the time of these early mass baptisms, and later as the 'Holy River of St Paulinus'. St Paulinus was a Roman missionary, and the first Bishop of York.

[19] Now known as Marne Barracks, it was opened in 1914 as a training base for the Royal Flying Corps, later the RAF.

From happy journeys such as this, I picked out a south facing dale longhouse high above the river Swale near Low Row.[20] This remote stone sanctuary, nestled on a throne of peatland beside a larch ribboned gill, was where I imagined I would live one day with my sheepdog. This was the top of the world; it encompassed everything with which I was familiar.

I am like wool caught on a barbed wire strand, like a shelf of carboniferous rock smoothed by the swift and ceaseless flow of unbroken time.

My soft backed atlas held endless fascination. Sitting in our chilly North Riding farmhouse the tantalising names of Srinagar, Sahara, Mississippi, Ceylon, excited the imagination. School projects on Egypt and Cambodia introduced the Middle East and Asia. If life was grounded in rural Yorkshire, the colours of countries danced over the pages of my imagination. The UK was the green of fresh spring grass; China, daffodil yellow; the USSR, a fearful red; and India, a mysterious and heady lilac. The complexity of late 1960s politics drifted over me; student unrest, the Vietnam and Cold wars, all stirred the wireless in a monotone of grey voices, but my sense of the wider world was a rainbow stretching across the bookshelf in my bedroom.

Life may have been a sea of ships sailing in and out of our vision, but we remained islanders, detached, sheltered by cows and sheep, potatoes and barley.

§

A schoolfriend's father worked in Yemen. I was fascinated by her worldliness in comparison to my own limited experience. Caroline wore silver jewellery bought from souks in Aden, scarves dyed in flamboyant pinks and reds that suited her small, blonde, bobbed frame; she smelt heady with musky perfume. My young mind delighted in her flamboyance and our conversations often touched on her travels.

'Where are you going to this school holiday?'

'Mum and I are flying to Dubai. Dad will come over to meet us.'

---

[20] Traditional dales farmhouses have one long roof covering a barn for the cattle and the family home in a semi-detached arrangement. This style of dwelling was modelled on ideas brought over by Nordic settlers. Converted, or dilapidated, they are a testament to a farming life that has now largely been assigned to the history books.

I had never been on a aircraft, although my father pointed out Concorde when it rumbled overhead one day; up to this point no one in our family had ever flown.

'Dubai?'

'Yes, it's just a road beside the Gulf really, with one or two hotels.'

Hotels were alien concepts and I knew nothing of the word Gulf. I looked lost.

'The Persian Gulf. A sea, silly.'

Once more I was embarrassed by my limited knowledge. In a few visits made to the North Sea at Saltburn and Whitby I associated the coast with being a wind-raking snarl of shoreline. My only acquaintance with Persia was in the guise of *Aladdin*. The name Dubai sounded seductive. I noted that I must look it up in my atlas as I had no idea where it sat in comparison to the rest of the world.

'We've stayed there before,' Caroline continued, 'it's just a desert. There's nothing much around, a few souks. Oh, and plenty of goats and camels.'

'Camels!'

This was intriguing. There were camels in our school scripture books that wandered in and out of pictures of sand dunes and palm trees.

'And it's so hot there you can't stay outside for long, just a few minutes or you'll collapse.'

Listening to Caroline, it struck me how my parents would call it all too foreign.

Each summer there were a few hot days when my sister and I would lie towels out on our front lawn and sunbathe just like the young women in the adverts in our mother's *Woman's Own* magazine. But very warm days in Yorkshire were a rarity compared to the days we huddled into our anoraks against the chilly rain.

'So...is it much hotter than here?'

'Way hotter! The men wear long white dresses, like nighties, to keep cool.'

The menfolk of my acquaintance wore boiler suits over their thick cotton checked shirts and serviceable denim jeans to protect them from the abundance of muck and mud that stuck to them like iron filings to a magnet. White dresses were extraordinary, it was incredible to think of any man wearing one, especially my father and his friends.

'Crikey! They must look really weird.'

'Not really, when you've been there a while you get used to it. It's all so different...they eat things that you've never heard of. Like, hummus and machboos,[21] and camel's milk ice cream.'

'Yuk! Why don't they eat normal food?'

'And they eat things that are a bit like curry...'

Again, she noted my discomfort.

'You must have had an Indian before! From the take-out in town?'

I shuffled on my chair, completely out of my depth having had fish and chips once or twice from the shop near my grandmother's house.

'But they must have a roast on Sunday?'

She laughed.

'Nooo stupid. It's not England.'

After school I looked through my atlas, counting the countries and the seas my friend and her mother would have to fly over to reach Dubai. Father would often encourage us to count the county borders and the rivers we crossed all the way into Northumberland. The distance between our farm and the Arabian desert seemed too vast to contemplate. When Caroline talked about taking the train to London and flying from Heathrow, she had already entered the realms of the inconceivable.

I did not share this new-found interest in the Middle East with my sister. Instead, I scrutinised maps in the secrecy of our shared bedroom when she was not around. I liked to be alone when reflecting on the space that had unexpectedly opened between soil and soul.

We are all cartographers, drawing our own landscapes. We all walk the path on which the sun rises and sets and the moon pursues its lunar cycle. Every path possesses many identities. We may share a story, but it never travels the same road.

Decades later, I recall these schoolgirl conversations when my husband, Mo, and I move to Dubai for his work. Settling into city life, I am no longer an extension of an intimate landscape. The sediments of this city's concrete layers are deposited skywards, apartments above shopping malls, apartments above

---

[21] Hummus, along with many common dishes today, was unheard of at the time. Machboos is a spicy lamb and rice dish. Only the most basic spices, like cinnamon and nutmeg, were found in our kitchen cupboard and used in cakes. Rice was baked in the oven in milk and served as a pudding, never with savoury food. Foodstuff such as olive oil was confined to the first aid box for helping remove ear wax, cloves were also medicinal, used to relieve toothache.

hotels, above offices, above apartments. Yet in-between the rise and fall of Dubai's synthetic fells, the sun sets with an amber flourish on most days of the year, the sand steals back onto the city roads at every opportunity, the rhythm of the white-lit Persian Gulf parades its turquoise waves along the coastline, and the clarity of the night sky enriches darkness with a wealth of millions of stars.

For centuries, the Bedouin have inhabited this peninsular, moulding their lives into the natural cyclical pattern of this arid desert region. When travelling outside of Dubai city occasional traditional camel farms huddle into the landscape on the arterial roads. In the desert, waves of tarpaulin are stretched on poles over shared living space providing shade from the searing sun for both humans and animals, the same principle of shelter as a dale's longhouse.

In London, before flying out to Dubai, Mo and I are given cultural training. A map of the world is unfurled before us. The contours are disorientating. This map appears skewed. In the centre lies the Middle East. The British Isles are on the periphery of the page. It reminds us that we are fragments, flotsam, floating in and out of how we perceive ourselves and how others see us.

Although our corner of Yorkshire appears rooted and timeless and every rock, upland and woodland, seems to defy movement, this landscape is lapping against change. Features in the land tell of human development: the rig and furrow ploughing system;[22] the round sunken bell-pit depressions pocking the fells where once shafts were sunk for mining;[23] or the hushes on the surface that scar the moor in gorged channels.[24]

In contrast, the natural world controls its own maps, shifts with its own momentum: in the paddle of cattle across meadows; boundaries of sheep hefts;[25] the extensive system of rabbit burrows; the trail of a badger under the cover of darkness; the threads between fungi and tree roots in symbiotic coexistence under the surface of the earth.[26]

---

[22] Parallel ridges and troughs originated from the open field system of farming used in the Middle Ages.
[23] An early method of extracting minerals that lay close to the surface of the land. A shaft and a bell chamber would be dug underground from which miners would winch the coal, galena (lead), or ore formed in the rock, up to the top.
[24] Hushing was a method of releasing water dammed at the top of the moor to wash away the topsoil in channels and expose the veins of minerals underneath. Hushes are still clearly visible in Swaledale.
[25] Sheep hefting is the term used for the intrinsic knowledge of belonging on the unfenced fells passed down through generations of ewes to their lambs.
[26] Known as mycorrhizas.

Oystercatchers map their way back to the riverbanks of the Swale, arriving each spring having abandoned their coastal winter-feeding grounds. Their vivid orange bills muster a commotion as they prattle 'peet-peet' and settle in like tourists on a package holiday.

Choirs of bright bills, busy over mud banks, touch a belonging, a gentle pulling together of offcomers, wanderers, flying back and forth, sharing the season. The door of their river home always open, a summer house, a kitchen table, a spare room for a friend.

Early May brings the cuckoo's return to the Swale Gorge from an African winter.[27] The natural auditorium of limestone enhances the onomatopoeia of their song as it bounces off the rock with a sharp, unerring 'cuck...kooo cuck... kooo cuck...kooo'. Hearing the first call of the season generates a sizzle of electricity, a connection between human and bird. But the cuckoo cannot be anthropomorphised. It defies sentimentality in the parasitic manner it lays its egg in another bird's nest and then abandons any notion of looking after its own young. This may seem callous, but for the purpose of reproduction it is successful.

We may pause in our everyday comings and goings, embrace the birdsong, imagine the connection between our cognitive senses and other species with which we share this earth. But the limitations of being human should never be underestimated in comparison to the intrinsic qualities that are mapped into nature to ensure its survival. Nature is fluid and independent. Natural is a term we use to essentialise behaviour; the term *natural world* weighted with meaning limited to human understanding of nature.

We carry conceptual maps inside us, but these landscapes rub alongside absences and edges, imagination and reality.

Physical maps are fixed in a moment of time, out of date before they are printed. A map is a gap through which the truth will fall.

---

[27] The name given to the valley through which the River Swale flows between Muker and Keld.

ROOTS
'deep roots are not reached by the frost'[28]

Old farming families are rooted into their land. Like plants, they inhabit the surface of the earth, dependent on the top few inches of soil to sustain them. But the living land, the organic matter on which existence is shaped is a product of rock far beneath the surface and remains largely invisible. Limestone and shale flavour the air and the water that runs through the dales and thus the vegetation that grows on them. Milk and cheeses are defined by the mosses and grasses that thrive on this millennia of alkaline soils from which the animals feed.

The grey cobble stones used to build traditional dales housing are as characterful as the climate that moulds and defines people and place. This is an environment that births hardened folk with stoical attitudes, resilient and resourceful. There is a sense of privilege to be so close to a place that you can feel the heartbeat; an intense and deeply intimate familiarity that moves between the body, mind and environment.

At a tired wicker gate, slouching against a drystone wall,[29] a short-flagged path leads down to an 18th century farmhouse in which my great-grandparents have lived all their married lives and my great-great-grandparents before them. A solid oak door has warped in its dressed stone frame, made long ago when the population was much shorter in height. It stops the path in its tracks at the entrance to a back kitchen: dusty Yorkshire sandstone lies underfoot. To the right, beside a scratched pot sink ingrained with dirt impossible to scrub clean, there is a stone shelf on which potatoes, onions and leeks wait to be cleaned for cooking. Oil-skin coats, heavy with winter, hang expectant of shorter days, their aroma of cattle heightened by a gust of late heat. On the pantry's cool marble top a cured ham rests under a wire dome. A metal-netted safe stands underneath, guarding freshly made curd tarts[30] from bluebottles and flies. Through an open door, a range blasts with heat needed to boil water. Bread is baked daily in the oven that nestles within its black frame; cleaned once a week with baking soda and vinegar. The room is brown: a robust pine table and two

---

[28] J.R.R. Tolkien.
[29] Built without mortar from stones gathered off the land and from small quarries, drystone walling is a centuries old craft, passed down through generations of countryfolk.
[30] Curd is coagulated milk, a by-product of cheesemaking. Traditionally made at Whitsuntide, the recipe used up the curds so as not to waste any food stuff. This rustic tart is a shortcrust pastry case filled with a mixture of fresh cheese curds, eggs, butter, sugar, currants, nutmeg.

dressers stand alongside walls, doors and skirting boards all painted the same practical shade. The whole appearance is as solid and as sedimentary as the worn slabs on which we walk.

Farming families are aware their tenure is brief, that their legacy will continue to be cultivated long after they are gone.

'Live as though you will die tomorrow, farm as though you will live forever.'

This was a common saying amongst the elders in my youth.

§

In 2011 we move into Reeth.[31] Here, offcomers are tolerated, but not without first answering questions about their origins. Soon after arriving an older resident corners me:

'Ar' thee local lass?'

'Yes I am. I was brought up on a farm five miles from Richmond.'

'Nay. Thee's not local if thee's frum Richmun'.'

'Well, my great-grandmother was an Alderson by birth.'

'Yer not kidding! By heck.'

His ruddy face reflects for a moment or two, then he gives a nod in silent approval, for he knows as well as I that in this part of the world family names hold clout; the name of a place or farm often reflects that of a clan.

'Do thee know, al' the Aldersons[32] in the world trace themselves back to Arkengarthdale.'[33]

When I next visit the village post office another elder of the village flashes a beaming smile at me, addressing the entire queue waiting to be served:

'This lady's one of us thee knows.'

'Aye, she's an Alderson.'

The name generates ripples of approval across the gathered. I am kin and as such I have earned my place on their map.

---

[31] The principal settlement in Swaledale, approx. 10 miles west of Richmond, North Yorkshire.
[32] The truth of his statement is open to question but often quoted as fact in the area.
[33] Arkengarthdale is a dale of four miles that runs north-west of Reeth.

A grey-haired, straight-skirted lady catches me at the front of my house. Authority is easily read into her manner. She has come with further news of my roots.

'I've been looking you up.'

I thank her for her time and interest.

'See over there. Bleak House. Out on its own over on the fell.'

Standing in our south facing garden, I look over to Harkerside where her wagging finger points.

'Yes, I think so.'

'Well, that's where your lot used to farm. Your line comes from yonder. Christopher. Your great-grandmother died giving birth to your grandmother, a rum do, but fairly common. So, he married his sister-in-law, your great-aunt Elizabeth. Happened a lot then, death I mean. Which meant an unmarried relative would come to look after the baby and the other children if there were any. Then, before you knew it, she was wife number two, or even three. All this inter-marrying makes tracing them all back so difficult.[34] Alderson genes tie this dale in knots.'

I feel my imagination leap towards the dwelling on the hillside. It stands apart, as lonely as the name suggests, where the cantankerous sky and the horizon clash on most days of the year. Bleak House is a compass, pointing to the generations to which I can now trace myself, reaching far into the 1700s. From this discovery I uncover further farmsteads linked to my ancestral past:

Bones of beginnings rest between Low Cringley[35] and today: slack-backed limestone, chert-ground, roofless ruins, blood-mapped, fashioned into family, faceless names in worn graves of walls; ancestors keep their centuries close. Overgrown and weather-fallen, nature re-aligns, slowly writing us out of our story.

We are given an original watercolour of the vista from a ridge close to Downholme,[36] looking west towards Marrick in Swaledale, painted by a local Victorian artist, Jessie Joy. It is dated 1852, but the view is as familiar in the 21st century as it was for Jessie. In winter light, standing on the spot where she

---

[34] There is an Alderson society *afhs.org* and the Upper Dales Family History Group, *upperdales.weebly.com* for anyone interested in tracing ancestors.

[35] Low Cringley, is a ruined farmstead on Reeth Low Moor, once farmed by my Alderson ancestors.

[36] Downholme is a hamlet of less than twenty stone built cottages, and a pub, crouched on a fellside equidistant between Reeth, Leyburn and Richmond.

must have set her easel down, my eyes sketch the uplands and the liquid sky that stagnates over afternoons at this time of year. Although I know nothing of Jessie other than our shared love of this view, there is a companionship, despite living our lives one hundred and seventy years apart.

The geology of Swaledale is a psychological haven where my own scant presence is urged into a search for permanence. Standing at Jessie's spot evokes a sense of spirituality; I am absorbed into the earth's biological clock, subsumed beyond a time that has any relevance to my day. It is reassuringly affirming; feels like a pilgrimage.

Over the next few months, I continue to find relatives that surprise and delight, discovering I am descended from the Raw family, the Quaker brothers George, Leonard and John, through my maternal great-grandmother's father. The Raws founded the first school in Reeth, the Friends Endowed, in 1778.

Grit stone, grit lives, layered into the gut of this land. Raised in their hands, pick, shovel, rake. The path came first, stone flags like impostors, one by one, as if lives were dependent on them. Then the Quaker men, building with books, placing chalk into the hands of children; reading the present, writing the future.

Today, a stone flagged path wanders westwards along Back Lane is all that remains of the site. In stumbling upon this information, I connect with the men, women and children who once walked this path to the school as though they were beside me, prodding my shoulder at the shop counter to tell me we too are related.

My roots are settling into the fissures in the land. In these folds of fellowship, the rhythm of vastness is awakened to the fraying lichen thriving on a thumb of stone, a black beetle rambling through fog-grass, the neat earth-holes of the field vole. I feel a belonging; so small and everywhere; it fills my belly.

Home is in the first sighting of the conifer copse shaped like a ship on top of Stainton Moor; the distant silver light of Semerwater[37] that mirrors the sky from the highest ground between Grinton and Redmire; the silhouette of Pen Hill rising between Coverdale and Wensleydale. On these moors, the pink hue of a summer evening never forgets to warm the stone scars with rose; late

---

[37] Semerwater is the second largest natural lake in the Yorkshire Dales, Malham Tarn being the largest.

autumn mists can cling obstinately to the river. Here, bright light hails rain, cows know to move down onto lower pastures and sheep seek shelter against drystone walls. All this is the result of millions of years of evolution. If a local cannot remember your grandparents, or has not heard tell of your great-grandparents, or you have no relations buried in the layers of the churchyard, then you can only ever be an offcomer.

PLACE
'Pass those names across your tongue as though they were poems'[38]

Prospect Hill Farm was once part of the Brough Hall Estate. On 19th June 1919, several farms were sold off and bought by the local council to provide opportunities for soldiers returning from WW1 who wanted to farm. A copy of the sale catalogue is still in our family. It is an archive, a manuscript. It weaves the story of a way of life that has passed beyond living memory between each page. Descriptions of the acreage, farmsteads and farmhouses, provide a fascinating foray into the history of both farming and domestic life in the last two centuries.

Eighteen lots of fertile farms, compact, straight fenced and desirable: valuable pasture, sound arable, stock raising, corn growing, rich with grazing.

Growing timber all included, large, covered cattle folds,[39] fowl houses, trap houses, hay houses, root houses, engine rooms, stackyards and stables for cart horses, pigsties, bullock sheds, loose boxes, granaries, lofts and good dry yards.

Blacksmiths' shops, small-holdings, superior farmhouses, substantial cottages and capital stone homesteads.

Houses with dining rooms and withdrawing rooms, dairies, kitchens, sculleries, cellars, wash houses, coal houses, wood houses, outhouses, cheese rooms, churning rooms, box rooms, storerooms, backyards, fold yards, front gardens, kitchen gardens with walls of mature bush fruit.[40]

Prospect Hill Farm, like other farms on the estate, was divided into two after it was sold: Prospect Hill, and Prospect Farm, the latter was ours. Both farms were relatively small and by the 1980s had become unviable under modern farming practices. The fifty-two acres we farmed necessitated taking summer grazing for the youngest heifers[41] to supplement the grass we needed for the

---

[38] Andrew Greig, *At The Loch Of The Green Corrie.*
[39] An enclosed yard for holding cattle within the farmstead.
[40] All references taken from the original sales catalogue.
[41] A heifer is not a cow until she gives birth to her second calf.

dairy cows and haymaking. The animals were taken off the farm in May and moved to fields we rented for the summer months, returning at the end of September.

The grazing my father took was close to the small market town of Masham, about twelve miles from home. Because the stock had to be monitored weekly, this meant Sunday mornings were spent accompanying him to see the cattle whilst my mother cooked lunch. We usually stopped in Masham marketplace for ice cream on the way to the land; a treat my father insisted we kept to ourselves. On our return journey, we would wind down the car windows and let the wind gurn our faces shapeless whilst the radio bellowed out the latest hits: Suzi Quatro, Wizzard, Slade, or best of all, *Blockbuster* by Sweet.

For successive years, this summer grazing was shared with a neighbour, Tommy. It was here I first tried my hand at driving. Although some years from being able to drive legally, I was used to taking out my father's little grey Fergie[42] now and then when help was needed. Tractors were numb beasts in the days before hydraulic steering, so heavy feet and strong arms were needed to haul the weight of their bodies around fields when collecting hay bales or transporting fodder out to the sheep in winter.

Tommy was a die-hard Yorkshire man with the broadest of local accents that rolled off his tongue like treacle.

'Dust thee know a've nivver been outta Yorkshire boy nor man?'

This was a fact that he was enormously proud of in his inimitable jovial manner. His beaten and ruddy complexion sat between feathers of silver whiskery sideburns which dressed his cheeks; he was the hardiest of northern men.

When we were young, he and his family moved from a village near the local market town of Bedale to the farm bordering our land on the eastern side. The first time we met he insisted on calling me Judith and eventually I plucked up courage to correct him, something my parents had not done. He then proceeded to call me Julie. Finally, after another correction, we settled on Ju.

One Sunday I accompanied my father and Tommy to the land at Masham. Tommy, eager for a bit of fun, pointed to the driver's seat of his dilapidated dark green van used as a farm workhorse:

'Dust thee want to have a go at't wheel Ju?'

---

[42] Grey Fergie's were the beloved Ferguson TE20 tractor, the workhorse on most farms up until the last decades of the 20th century. Some still survive today. They were manufactured for a decade after the war, between 1946 and 1956, and often the first piece of modern machinery a farmer introduced onto his farm.

To pass your driving test was the primary aim of most teenagers who lived in our outlying communities and coveted as the window of freedom from which we could fly.

'Haw-way then, in yer get.'

The functional motor smelt of cattle; the dashboard was thick with dust from last year's harvest. Abandoned sweet wrappers and packaging from animal medicines scattered the ripped leather bench seat that spewed felted innards. A rolled newspaper, weeks old, faded and yellowing, was used to swat flies on the windscreen as he drove. There was enough straw in the foot-well to bed a calf pen; overall, a typical farmer's run-around.

Tommy was a man with a story for every occasion and they were always told with a glint of mischief and a chuckle:

'Do thee know Ju; I once knew a farmer who 'ad a Mini. He was so tall he took front driver's seat owt and sat in't back seat so he could reach pedals wi'owt getting cramp.'

'Aye, he got sum q'weer looks frum those that didn't know 'im.'

'An' then he goes an' marries a slip o' a lass that doesn't even cum up to his armpits. She sits so far in front of 'im in passenger seat it looks like she's the one that's driving, even though she's sat on't wrong side.'

'Police stopped 'em one day and the pair of 'em had to go to the station to explain. They thawt they wor messing about summit terrible. A proper danger to themselves and others.'

I had no such problems and jumped straight into the driver's seat. Even at fourteen, this was not an invitation to pass up, especially when my father was out of sight and preoccupied with mending a fence.

The van was as supple as a ballet dancer in comparison to our tractor. This was swiftly confirmed as we hurtled across the field towards a hawthorn hedge at a speed I had no idea how to control.

'Brake lass brake. Use yer brake. Braaaake.'

'Which one's the brake?'

'Nay, not thatun!'

He reached over to grab the steering wheel forcing a swerve sideways into the hedge-back to avoid the impact of a head-on collision.

'Is this the brake?'

I hit the pedal with a neck-wrenching jolt just as we turned. Saving himself from being launched through the windscreen, Tommy took a moment to sort his breathing out after we had come to a halt.

'Aye lass, remember thee needs to know where't brake is in life as well as't accelerator. Thee nivver knows when thee's going t'need it.'

My first driving lesson was concluded with this positive piece of advice.

Back at home we laughed as we recounted the near miss to my mother:

'Well! I've never heard the likes. Driving! She's much too young for that. What were you men thinking?'

Tommy scurried away before she could say anything more to him, leaving my father like a naughty schoolboy. Then, turning to me:

'You can forget driving lessons for another three years my girl. Where was your father when all this was going on?'

§

Although the farms in our community were no longer part of Brough Hall after the sale of the estate, traditions were less easy to sever. The late Baronet's family maintained a commitment to their former estate tenants. All who farmed the land sold off decades earlier were invited to his daughter's wedding in 1962; my parents attended, taking me in my pram.

Every Christmas a member of the family would visit all the farms with the gift of a bottle of whisky for each household. Some years this meant children accompanied their parent. Often this was a young girl who was a similar age to me.

Politeness meant our visitors would be invited to step indoors and led through the kitchen and into our living room. Never accepting a seat, they hovered just inside our small, cramped room where a serviceable sofa, two large leather armchairs and an oak dining table, which had belonged to my father's family, filled the room. On the large table my mother made our clothes, her Singer sewing machine spending days perched at one end when she was running us up a new pair of trousers, or a skirt. Here we did our homework, my father spread *The Farmer's Guardian* newspaper every Friday to read from front to back, and various letters and paperwork often sat waiting to be transferred to his writing desk.

I would nonchalantly scrutinise our guests with purposeful detachment, not wanting to appear too interested. Likewise, the young girl tried to disguise her curiosity, but her eyes betrayed an inquisitiveness as they scouted the room. I remember squirming when they landed on me. I noted the outward signs of economic difference, self-conscious for the first time. The squire-suited gentleman with the petite blond girl, gathered up into the most luxurious cream fur collared coat, spoke to me starkly of disparity. But it was her hair that transfixed me; long and soft around her fine-boned cheeks. In her presence I was conscious of my own big-boned frame, of which my grandmother reminded me so often, and the practical short back and sides haircut my mother kept on top of with her eager scissors.

'Are you a boy?'

A young girl had once asked me this in the playground after one of my mother's attempts at cutting my hair. I shrank into my duffle coat and vowed to myself that when I was old enough to choose I would have long hair so no one would ask me such a question again.

Under the quiet censorship of this perfect girl, I felt uneasy. Father and daughter highlighted the basic functionality of the room and I did not like the scrutiny one bit.

'Where will you spend Christmas?'

My mother made small talk as I retreated further into myself.

'Oh, we are back from London now so all the family will gather up here.'

When in the north they lived in a Georgian house sited on the estate. The Hall had stood empty in the years since the death in 1973 of the previous incumbent; the fate of many large properties.[43]

Even as a child I envied this family their ability to trace their ancestry back through history and not have to piece together their past like a jigsaw. I had already experienced the urge to understand my own story through those who had lived before me as I studied old photograph albums at my grandmother's house.

As the adults' chatter was coming to a natural end, I gave the girl a sideways glance and she mirrored one back at me as she left the room. Did I sense a slight air of superiority in this gesture? I had willed them to leave, and my mood did not recover quickly after they had gone.

---

[43] A few years later the Hall was converted into leased apartments.

Subsequently, after one of these Christmas visits, I questioned my mother about the differences in their clothes and speech.

'We have our place and they have theirs.'

Her reply perpetuated my uneasy response to their visit:

'Just remember, if you'd been born a hundred years ago, you'd be a servant working in their kitchens by now my girl.'

To my young bookish mind, constantly expanding with ideas to take me beyond the farm, the horror of this notion rippled inwardly. I was aware that our lives seemed as static as those of our grandparents, and their parents before them; perpetuated in the pattern of our working hours, the food we ate; habitual and constant. Whenever I queried why we did something in a particular way the reply was fired back:

'You do as I say because I'm your mother.'

Another frequent response was:

'Because we do things the right way here. The way they've always been done.'

And most often:

'It makes sense.'

My parents constantly reinforced wisdom drawn from their known way of doing things.

As teenagers in a hurry to grow up, the appreciation of our rural hill-top home, detached from the nearest village by a mile of fields, gradually waned. We began to crave shops, the youth club discos and the bus service into town.

With hindsight, home was a nurturing environment, with freedom to wander and observe the world around us; beside becks, in ancient woodlands, along hedge-backs where primroses closed their petals in the rain and stars lit the beech trees on cloudless twilight evenings. How the undulating fields concealed small scoops of land where frost lingered longest on harsh short-shadowed winter days. To know and feel the skin and flesh of a place so intimately was a blessing. These riches jewelled the world we were born into and, for most of childhood, compensated for much that might niggle a questioning mind.

§

Sitting in a cave buried in the uplands near Pateley Bridge, our class of sixteen-year-olds were at the end of compulsory education. The limestone was tightly bound around our young bodies as we all squeezed into a coffin-sized space together. Every nerve and sensation accentuated, pulsing; my heart chimed an anxious bell in my ears.

'Where do you want to find yourself in five years' time?'

The young teacher's voice was disorientating, coming to us through the absolute blackness in the hollow of rock we sat inside under Nidderdale. I felt a sense of being a conduit, absorbing the sound waves of his voice as it bounced off the bowels of this alien underworld. When he fell silent, only the slow drip of water edged into the arena his words vacated. Such a languid, hypnotic drop echoed so loud it was as though it touched every rock face that surrounded us. Then, once again he broke the spell, his words spilling out like a genie from a lamp:

'Be brave in your choices. Push the boundaries of yourself if you want a fulfilling life. Don't live in darkness, have confidence to walk unfamiliar paths, even when you can't see where they may lead.'

'Isn't this the opposite to my parents' advice', I remarked to myself as he fell silent.

Even now his voice persists in my head. I still believe I must trust the tracks that lead me away from that cave; battle challenges full on.

As a youngster, I was learning about life second hand as I sat beside the hearth in the core of our farmhouse listening to the adults endless talk about the state of farming; nothing else seemed to matter. I remember watching them with the sense that I had sat there for centuries, listening to the same stories, same concerns. On these occasions the past weighed over me like a heavy jacket, buttoning me so tight it was harder and harder to wear as my growing frame reached into adolescence.

§

The farm was a presence, a character that dominated, was both master and servant, demanding and giving. Graced with original one storey stone buildings, there were two yards, both as clarty[44] as each other, extending to the west of, and perpendicular to, our square brick farmhouse built around 1920. Nearest the house, the lower yard was large enough for several vehicles and accommodated the main cow byre and dairy, a small building known as the pig hole, a hay barn, the cattle collecting yard and, on its northern border an aged

---

[44] Muddy.

creosoted single wooden garage that lounged slightly off kilter, daring a keen wind to blow it over.[45]

Prospect Hill Farm and Prospect Farm taken in July 1975. The original farmhouse in the foreground belongs to Prospect Hill Farm, our house is set back from the main farmstead a little. Note the vein-like cattle tracks in the field behind. Summer meant the cows habitually travelled the same routes, back and forth twice a day to be milked.

To the left of the garage ran a wall westwards. Here, a small incline met a newly built bullpen. Another dirt-trodden ascent passed through a gate leading to the upper yard, known as the stackyard. A block wall on the right was part of the purpose-built indoor cubicle house for the cows, erected when a scattering of small byres was replaced by the parlour. We kept rabbits in a home-made hutch on this outer wall. At one time a wild rabbit must have got into this hutch and mated with our tame ones. Consequently, a line of near uncatchable off-spring sent us daily in to our mother scratched, bitten and bleeding.

'I hate those rabbits!'

'You'll have to get rid of them Robbie.'

'Aye'

---

[45] Eventually it did collapse and was replaced with an open-fronted breeze-block shed.

In response, my father could often coax anyone who peered into the hutch: 'Take the lot if you like.'

Two sides of the upper yard[46] were formed by a huddle of old-fashioned store houses, one of which was used as a calving pen, others as wintering sheds, which, at lambing time, would be lined with straw bales to create draft-free birthing rooms. A wooden hen house in the centre of this yard interrupted the view across to a Dutch hay barn,[47] which formed the westerly edge; behind the henhouse stood a stone granary[48] with tread-worn stairs to the first floor that graced the outside of the wall. Off the creosoted rail-lined balcony at the top, a solid door led into a room where the barley would be stored after harvest. This external balcony also provided a complete view of the inner sanctuary of this garth,[49] like looking over onto the cloisters of an abbey.

Straight uphill, behind the Dutch barn[50] was a tractor house hidden in a small, neglected paddock where bits of machinery, which might come in handy one day, were kept. This assortment of rusty twisted metal attracted the scrap men with keen eyes that missed nothing when they came calling. Here the air loitered, spilling over our heads with a porous odour of oil and diesel which only an occasional animal smell could penetrate. Like both yards below, nothing underfoot was concreted. The churn of muck was the inevitable consequence no matter how much my father shovelled and cleaned the ground in a daily ritual. It was not until into the 1970s that the lower yard was given a hardcore surface, the upper part of the farmstead was never tidied in the same manner. Cost was the constant issue and a deterrent to such improvements.

In contrast, the farmhouse was fronted by my mother's neat flower garden and bordered on one side by a mown drying green, complete with a wooden hut like a bothy that we called the playhouse. At the back a sloping concrete yard bumped into the coal house at the bottom. This had once been the outside closet in the days before internal plumbing. Close by, a long wooden calf house had been erected in the corner of the field next to the drying green, with the added advantage of giving the farmhouse welcome protection from north-east winds in winter. Two hen houses perched on bricks in the same field.

---

[46] Old English 'geard', an enclosed area.
[47] Old English 'bereaern', a storage space for barley.
[48] Latin 'granarium', a store for threshed grain.
[49] Old Norse 'garor', meaning enclosure, later garden.
[50] Dutch barns are post-framed barns that became popular in the 19th century for storing hay and straw.

The gate to all our land sat adjacent to the rear of the house and this was where the cows assembled when they were ready for milking in summer. Farm animals and humans lived in proximity, aware of each other and dependent on each other. Passing by after milking, the nosier members of the herd would stop and peer in through the living room window, attracted by the flashing colours of the television, moving on when their inquisitiveness was sated.

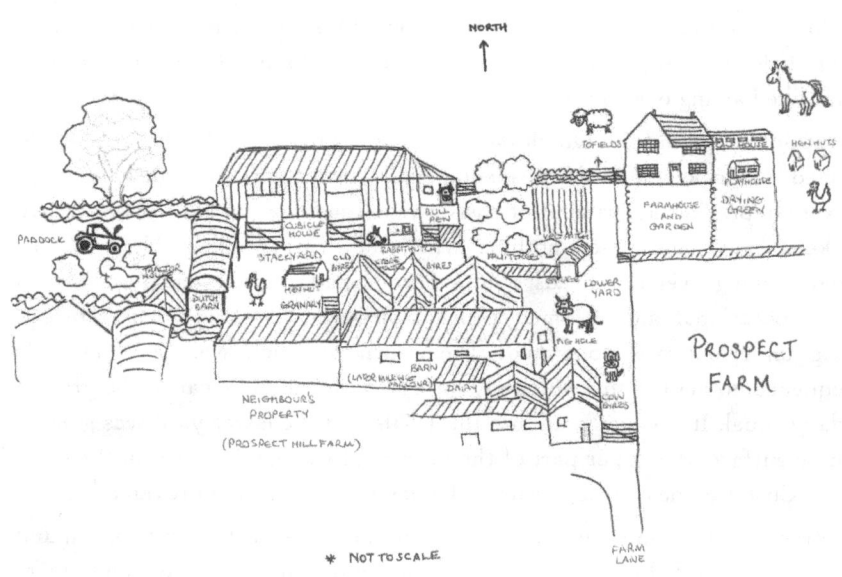

An illustration of the layout of our side of the farm. The division of the buildings was made when Prospect Hill Farm was sold in 1919. Our farm comprised of buildings to the back and eastern side of the original farmstead.

Wintertime often meant the bony black and white Friesians hung around, hunched up against the cold, waiting until their byres were hurriedly mucked out and they were once more returned to the comfort of warm, dry stalls to chew their cud. Winter meant backbreaking and unrelenting work for my parents; seven days a week the alarm clock shattered the dark shadows of my father's sleep. He would rise to start work pre-dawn, and not finish until long after the daylight had disappeared.

I remember confiding to my father one evening after school that I was worried about a spelling test.

'What do you need to worry about', he sighed as he measured calf-nuts into a bucket.

'Just wait until you're grown up, then you'll know what worry is.'

'Is that because there's no electricity half the time?'

'Aye. Power cuts divvent help.'

Frequently we sat in blackness through the winter months of 1973 into 1974, crouched around the open fire in our living room to keep warm. For emergencies my mother kept a flat-bottomed kettle that would sit on the hot embers in the fire and omit a continuous shrill whistle as it came to the boil. During industrial disputes and power cuts, dusk meant oil lamps and candles. Bedtime became a game of who could scare the others most, pointing out shadows on the staircase walls and unexplained creaks as the house sighed and settled down for the night. But our fears were soon distracted by the cold as we climbed into inhospitable beds in an arctic bedroom, clutching hot water bottles as we dived under the blankets to warm up.

Our parents tried to hide from us anything that worried them, but with hindsight I know most businesses were under duress in the 1970s, with inflation out of control and bank loan rates above 15%. At the time, anxieties about the economic viability of the farm were just snippets of overheard conversations. The overriding factor that seemed to anger both parents was wastefulness.

'Don't put anything on your plate you can't eat.'

'Make sure you only run two inches of water in the bath.'

'I'm not getting the car out just to go and buy you a box of Sugarpuffs.'

We knew nothing of the economics of life other than the pocket money we earned by mucking out cow byres at the weekend. After we had finished our jobs, despite washing wellies and scrubbing hands, our skin seemed to have absorbed the scent of cattle into every pore. The ritual of Sunday bath night was an important part of the weekend.

We not only lived alongside our ponies, dogs, sheep, cows, rabbits, chickens, but the blackbirds, rooks, and owls, the bees that swarmed the lilac tree in May, the crayfish we caught in the beck. We played hide and seek in and around the farm buildings, built dens in haystacks and followed ancient trails to derelict buildings that spooked us. There was an awareness that some friends led vastly different lives, with paper rounds, Saturday jobs in Woolworth's in Richmond;

or had fathers that were away for long stretches serving with the military, especially in Northern Ireland. They also had relatives that were scattered across far flung regions of the UK, including London, or abroad in Germany or Cyprus, whereas all our kin lived on farms they had been born on, or if not, remained in the localities of Yorkshire and Northumberland.

I never envied the lives of friends; home was a different country from theirs. In truth, our farmstead was a muddle of old-fashioned buildings built for a bygone era in agriculture and just about made do. Jumbled together with a few recently constructed additions, it was all that my parents had to sustain a practical living. Life in this weathered outpost was tough and when the easterlies blew in from Scandinavia, or Siberia, pummelling the house, it was tougher still. Only in my teens did I begin to understand my parents' years of struggling with money that had wilfully frustrated and dictated their existence.

But no matter what time of the year visitors drove into the farmyard, there was a consensus:

'Look at those views. Priceless.'

SEASONS
'Gone yesterday here tomorrow'[51]

Not long after the turn of the year the first visitors raise their white pearl-heads with hope; snowdrops greet the metal air, as they lighten heavy days.

Who brings this feast, brings these milk flowers that break the frozen ground; their slender arms offering shy prayers, to feed us with a quiet faith.

There was no central heating in our farmhouse. Winter was 'nitherin',[52] especially away from the open fire downstairs in the living room. Often, when we woke on a dark morning, we could run our fingernails down the ice that had formed on the inside of our bedroom windowpanes, ghost-writing on the glass before huffs of hot breath spirited our words away. Warmth was a luxury and complaints to my mother about the cold were met with a pragmatic solution:

'Put another jumper on.'

'But we're freezing.'

'Nonsense, go and play outside, then when you come back in, you'll feel the warmth.'

'I'm not putting any more coal on that fire.'

At the beginning of January, the cattle feed rep, fertiliser rep, and other company representatives, who called regularly at the farm throughout the year for my father's orders, were invited beyond the kitchen, into the living room. China plates and crystal glasses would be taken out of my mother's mahogany cabinet for the customary serving of sherry with a slice of Christmas cake, accompanied by a slither of Wensleydale cheese. My father would break off his outside jobs and come indoors to sit down with each of the men in turn as they called. This was not before he had been reminded by my mother to leave his wellies at the back door and carry a kitchen chair into the living room as he was never allowed to sit on the upholstery in work clothes. Inevitably the smells from the farmyard would penetrate the interior of the house, but dirt was banned from coming across the porch step, although wayward straw often left tell-tale signs of him passing through.

---

[51] M R Peacocke, *Thirteenth Night*.
[52] 'nitherin' is a Yorkshire dialect term for very cold.

All the reps were men. Negotiating prices and contracts with farmers was a gender-defined role. Women were considered, by most rural based companies, to be more suited to the office, typing-up invoices, answering phone calls and other administrative roles. The farm secretary was an exception to this rule. Trained at a local secretarial college, she would travel around the farms visiting each of her clients once a month to keep their accounts in order.

The cattle feed rep was the most frequent visitor to our farm. His chat, whatever time of the year, never strayed beyond the economy, market prices and cricket.

'All the best Robbie.'

This was the universal toast, followed by:

'Let's hope this one's a good year. Better than the last, hey?'

'I'll drink to that Fred.'

Both men would nod their heads, acknowledging their co-dependency, then take a sip of sherry, before falling into a moment of mutually supportive thought. There were many professions that depended on the other for their livelihoods in farming. But pessimism was most often the farmer's closest companion.

'I hope you've got a clean towel on that chair.'

My mother's voice interrupted from behind the kitchen door.

'Aye.'

'Look at all these bits you've brought in.'

'Aye'

'I've just brushed this kitchen floor. It's all over my lino.'

'Aye.'

Father would give a wink to his companion and smile. I noted how he relaxed in the presence of the men that visited. I also noticed the differences in the clothing each wore; my father's weathered complexion complimented his heavy cotton shirt that frayed at the collar with a threadbare jumper over the top held together by mending. In contrast, the neatly shaven rep looked dapper in his leather elbow-patched tweed jacket, corduroy trousers and polished brogues.

This ritual was followed one-by-one until all the reps had been received and paid their respects to my parents. Cake was held back if some had yet to call. Hungry fingers were tempted when rummaging through the pantry to sneak the last piece of the rich dark cake; but none of us dared take it, including my father.

When my siblings and I reached the last two years of primary school we were allowed to stay back for activities such as country dancing or sport, which meant we missed the bus and had to walk the mile home along Tunstall Road. One afternoon, returning alone, a car pulled up abruptly in front of me. I could barely see the profile of the man inside as he half-turned to look back at me. My mother's voice began drumming in my head as my heartbeat quickened:

'Don't get into a car with a stranger, even if they say they know your father or me.'

'If anyone stops, run away, don't approach the car.'

At the time this advice was given it slipped past me, but it must have been stored somewhere near the surface. There were high-profile cases of child abduction that had made the news headlines in the 60s and 70s, most notably the Moors Murders on Saddleworth.

Tragic cases of such children were often used to warn us of strangers. So, with these stories in mind, and without a moment of hesitation, I catapulted over the fence behind the car and into a field with young bullocks so startled they scattered. Running hard I reached safety behind a wide trunked ash, heaving frosty breath into the failing light of the afternoon like a chain smoker.

Gathering my wits and peering around the tree, much to my relief, the car engine could be heard speeding away up Petches Bank. I felt the tension of the narrow escape wain a little, whilst the bemused cattle stared at me, too interested to return to their fodder ring. Agitated, but out of danger, I began to tentatively retrace my steps. Then, with a swift clamber over the fence, I bolted towards home like an Olympic sprinter.

Entering the farmyard, I could see the car that had stopped me in my tracks was parked by the side of our house. Its occupant was nowhere to be seen, but a sudden wave of realisation washed over me and I guessed correctly, the fertiliser rep was inside our back porch chatting away to my father. I felt paralysed with embarrassment when I realised it was Jack, who I had known for most of my life. Flustered, all I could do was hide behind the metal water-butt in the drying green until he left.

Jack enjoyed a good chat, and my cover was eventually challenged by my mother who emerged from the house, having seen me fly past the kitchen window twenty minutes before. She was baffled:

'What are you doing? It's nearly dark!'

'Come in, now.'

'Honestly, I don't know what gets into you sometimes.'

Red-faced, from both my run and with self-consciousness, I crept out and skulked after her through the porch. Greeting me, Jack chirped:

'I think she's been practising cross-country.'

I could say nothing to counter his mirth and so darted upstairs, accompanied by my father's belly laughs as Jack retold the story of my dash. Later, when I finally came down from my bedroom, no one mentioned the incident. Episodes that might lead to a bit of teasing, or a good telling off, were sometimes unexpectedly brushed aside instead.

In the dark nights after Christmas and New Year, supper evenings were held by each of our farming neighbours in turn. This was a window of socialising for the adults, to help ease the dark cold days away before the work of another year began in earnest. When it was my parents' turn to host, we would be bundled off to bed early to listen to the adults below from our pillows. The muffled hum of chatter and laughter was a lullaby, we were safe in the good humour that permeated under the door from the bottom of the stairs.

Then, when I was nine or ten years old, I discovered amateur dramatics, although my mother might say this happened much earlier. I joined the Catterick Theatre Group and was given the role of a fairy in *Cinderella*, waving my wand and singing *Somewhere Over the Rainbow* along with a chorus of older girls. I was hooked.

Back at home, on rainy weekends, I directed my own productions, playing the lead role, with my two siblings and all the younger neighbouring children serving as bit part actors at my disposal. A bossy task master, I made them rehearse to within an inch of boredom before our performance in front of the few reluctant mothers we could muster.

Eventually, our show progressed to providing the entertainment for one of my mother's January evenings. Roles were polished, programmes artistically created, chairs set out and the table pushed to one side to make way. By the finale of an exhaustive medley of songs from the film *South Pacific*, including my gusto rendition of *I'm going to wash that man right out of my hair*,[53] the consensus from the audience was that 'there could be too much of a good thing'. Luckily for my mother, teenage angst was about to break out into tortuous self-consciousness and theatricals took on another guise.

§

---

[53] Rodgers and Hammerstein, 1949.

On the stage of a January moor top, ribbons of heat, pale pink, orange, violet, shift into the soliloquy of grey sky, smoke drifting in layers, like the limestone, gritstone and shale beneath the veneer of vegetation.

The wild uplands of the dales are as proactively managed as the lower fertile pastures that run along the valley bottoms. Once covered in forest, the land is now the product of man's intervention. Burning that takes place between October and April allows new green shoots of heather to regenerate in spring, eliminating older less nutritional, woody-stemmed plants. Hence, the moor is a patchwork of differing stages of re-growth feeding the grouse reared on these fells whilst providing cover for nesting birds in a diverse habitat of plants such as bog mosses, alpine pennycress and crowberry.

This practice has come under much analysis in the past decade by conservationists and there are many arguments that need to be acknowledged by those who manage the land. But landowners and gamekeepers, like farmers, maintain this is a working environment that supports the community on multiple levels including pubs, hospitality and local shops and is home to families that keep the local schools and businesses open, the countryside economically active.

The viability of country life is also challenged by the ownership of second homes and holiday cottages. If locals continue to be priced out of the property market it will decimate communities. There needs to be consideration given to a respectful balance between the population of the dales and the tourist industry.

§

On the farm we hibernated in winter. My father travelled no further than fifteen miles to the auction mart in Darlington on a Monday, or to Leyburn Mart on a Friday. Fodder was assessed regularly and worried over in terms of there being enough to feed the animals if spring was late, or if the fields were too wet to turn cattle out when planned. Everything was based on judgement and timing. Winter work was backbreaking and continuous; the mechanisation of farming was mostly beyond the pockets of our community of farms in the 1960s and 70s. The unrelenting cycle of a day - milking, feeding up, mucking out, milking again, feeding again - welcomed occasional moments of relief, often in the form of humour.

We kept a heavyweight boxer of a bull for breeding purposes. He lived in one of the smaller, converted stone byres behind a creosoted and patched up wooden door, much like a high stable door. His black and white head and pink wet nose, with a copper bull ring that was used to lead him when he was out of his house, could be seen moving back and forth with annoyance as he tried to peer over the top of the door when anyone walked into the stackyard, but especially at feeding time. Snorting his discontent, eager to be led out into the lower yard for exercise or for the business he was bred, the serving of cows.

One morning, he was tethered to a post whilst my father mucked his pen out when he seized the chance to slip his rope and go walkabout. Our neighbour, Joseph, was a great fixer and mender and would potter around doing odd jobs during the day. On this occasion he was intent on repairing the garden gate that led from his property onto our communal farm lane. As he worked away with the lane behind him, he felt a sudden puff of warm breath on the back of his neck.

'I turned around and jumped so bloomin' high I nearly left me boots behind.'

'He was stompin' and snortin' like he was fit to blow up.'

'Mark my words. I'm lucky to be here tellin' you this!'

Joseph stood on our doorstep hopping from foot to foot, not knowing whether to be angry or relieved for the safe deliverance from his encounter; unappreciative of the laughter that ensued as he told his tale.

'He was right there behind me, leanin' over to see what I was doin'.'

'I never heard him. I swear he tiptoed up to scare the livin' daylights out of me.'

My father pushed his flat cap back and scratched the top of his head to stem his mirth.

'Aye. Bull must have had a bigger shock when he saw it was you, Joseph.'

'You can laugh. You can laugh.'

'So, what did you do?'

By now we were all trying hard to keep our composure but Joseph was not laughing.

'What did I do? What did I doooo?'

'I cleared the ruddy wall from stand still, that's what I did.'

My parents collapsed at the image this conjured.

'You'll be enterin' point-to-point without a horse next. Let us know when and I'll make sure I put a shillin' on you.'

'Get away with you all. It could've been serious. What if he'd headbutted me, knocked me over, broken me back, killed me!'

'Howay Joseph, it'll take more than that young divel to finish you off.'

'I'm warning you Robbie. Get that animal behind a solid door afore there's a proper accident. He nearly stood on Tiny, 'til she told him where to go.'

Tiny was Joseph's appropriately named Yorkshire Terrier, a prima donna who went everywhere with him, riding on his knee with a stately air when he drove his car. With her fringe tied up in a red ribbon, she was the antithesis of a sheep dog. However, on this occasion she had proved her worth by standing her ground with resolve in telling this mighty bulk of beef to shove off.

'There's no denyin' Joseph. Today she's proved she's like the rest of the women round here,' my father chuckled.

In truth, when the panic spilled over the byre roof and into our yard, all work stopped in the rush to see what the uproar was about. There had been a moment, albeit fleeting, when my father had taken in the scene with concern. But having been used to the halter since he was a youngster, the bull was re-captured without fuss, and happy to be led away from his encounter with Tiny.

Soon after this fright a purpose-built bullpen was built, complete with an enclosed exercise yard, and no escape route. Joseph and Tiny were safe when mending fences and gates on the lane.

§

Humour diffused many situations; falling out was scarce and short-lived and after all, who would you talk to about the weather if you were not speaking to your neighbours.

It was always about weather. The winters your body dug itself into the snow to feed the sheep. Or heavy mornings, your head bowed, sunk into an overcoat against canes of rain, mud-damp bones calloused like limestone, the scent of livestock on leathered skin that mingled with petrolly, carbolic soap. How silence wrapped into the worn edges of you as we walked the sheep.

Weather preoccupied every adult in my childhood. They talked about it, cursed it, welcomed it, watched for clouds, for clear days, for signs of what it might bring, what it was like last year, what weather they needed that day, what they did not want next week, measured the rainfall and without fail listened to the forecast every evening on the wireless.

The tilt of the earth towards the spring equinox was an eagerly anticipated joy. From an early age, signs of spring were pointed out to us by our parents:

'Look, the birds are building their nests high this year.'

'It's goin' to be a fine warm spring.'

If the nests were built deeper down into the structure of the branches, then a wet spring with cool temperatures was predicted.

A spell of wintery weather often coincides with the blackthorn flowering. 'Beware the blackthorn winter,' rings true as late as April and May.

My father looked to the natural world for the signs of the weather to come:

'There'll be rain in a couple of hours when the air is as clear as this. You can see the Cleveland Hills today.'

'Rain before seven, fine by eleven.'

'The birds are flyin' way up, see if I'm not right, there'll be no rain today.'

'When the smoke from the chimney rises in a straight line, it is going to be fine.'

'A mornin' rainbow brings a warnin' of rain.'

'A snowy winter brings a good summer.'

Whenever we visited the seaside, we would bring home a length of seaweed and hang it on a nail outside the back door. If it turned soft and rubbery, rain was on its way; days when it was crisp meant no such downpours.

Nature provides for itself; a store of abundant haws and beech nuts means a hard winter is coming; moles will tunnel under hilly ground if a torrent of rain is about to fall and flood the lower levels; flower scent is stronger in moist air about to fall as rain; cows are known to sit with their faces into the wind; and at harvest time, tiny black thunder-flies mean exactly that.

A local amateur meteorologist was given the ear of the farming fraternity in Yorkshire and much respected for his weather predictions. In the 1830s his family had begun to keep records of rainfall, temperatures, and general notes on the day-to-day climate in Yorkshire. With this historical information at his disposal, he spoke of repetition in weather cycles over one hundred and seventy years. Like many country folks, he argued that plants, animals, and insects held a great deal of intelligence on climate and changes in patterns; this is now proven. He often contradicted the television weather-casters with his signposts such as frogs spawning in the middle of a pond. This, he said, heralded a droughty spring because frogs know that the edges of their ponds dry out without rain.

Our farming community was always hopeful for an early spring. When it did arrive, the greatest joy was to let out the stock from their winter barns onto fresh, new grass. There would always be a rush for release as gates opened and one after the other the cows and young stock tumbled with dizzying freedom into the fields, gulping the fresh air, clearing hay-dust from winter lungs. Older cows lumbered into a steady trot, udders swaying, whilst the heifers kicked hind legs up and stretched delighted limbs. Cattle are not animals of natural sprint, and so eventually, one by one they would steady to a walking pace, heads down, tongues curling the lush new shoots, pulling with a tear and grind, tear and grind. Sated, they sat in homely groups, easy with each other, chewing their cud in rhythmic motion, the sun a welcome warmth on their backs.

Every Easter my mother would boil hens eggs wrapped in the crisp outer skins of onions, tied inside balls of newspaper. She boiled the eggs hard and when cool unwrapped them to reveal rich mahogany, chestnut and cream swirls of colourings on the shells.[54]

On Easter Sunday we would go out into the Big Field to a short bank and standing at the top, roll our eggs down in competition to see whose egg would travel the furthest and survive the longest without cracking. Traditionally this symbolised the rolling away of the stones from Christ's tomb. For us, it was a game, the only significant event that marked Easter, other than a visit from family.

In the dales late spring is brimful of wildflowers with poetic names: Jack by the Hedge, Forget Me Not, Colt's Foot, Marsh Marigold, Bush Vetch and Lords and Ladies. Their giddy colours are reflected in a rainbow of fields. By May an electric Bluebell carpet sparks the old deciduous woodlands that line the lower banks of the dale. A galaxy of Ramsons[55] snag the air with their white-star petals and unmistakable pungency; shy pearls of pink Wood Sorrel bow whilst creamy-pink Hawthorn drapes its flush of bridesmaid-blossom over hedgerows. In these few weeks Swaledale is a garden.

Spring was the start of our picnic season. As a family, holidays were difficult to arrange because of the responsibility of milking twice daily and so a half-day Sunday outing up into Swaledale, taken now and then, was an adventure. We usually pitched up by the river Swale, on land owned by a friend of my father,

---

[54] Called 'pace' eggs from the word Passover.
[55] Wild garlic.

complete with fishing nets and jam jars, homemade orange juice and luncheon meat sandwiches. Here we would spend happy afternoons paddling, bent backed as we lifted stones carefully under the flow to catch a flash of minnows scooting across the riverbed in a blink. A bullhead was a prize catch; sporting an ugly wide head, this little fish was harmless but scary. All were returned to the river at the end of the day, but not before a count was taken to see who had netted the most.

Occasionally we ventured to Aysgarth waterfalls in Wensleydale, or to Brimham rocks in Nidderdale. This dramatic landscape of millstone grit deposits eroded by weather is littered with fantastically defiant forms. Stacked on ridiculously short narrow stumps sculpted by ice, rain and wind, dinosaurs and dragons perched as though they are about to topple; perfect for scrambling over. The rocks are given fantastical names: the Lizard's Footprint, Monster Stone and Crocodile's Head ignited our imaginations. We were trapped in a mythical kingdom between Middle Earth[56] and the heights of Yorkshire.

§

On the farm, haymaking, Wimbledon and gooseberries were interminably linked. The gooseberries grew near an old limestone quarry, planted by the hands of someone who cultivated the land before living memory. Hanging from the bushes like the earrings off my young teacher's ears, their rough, hairy bodies and unforgiving thorns, were cruel to our fingers. They tangled around bare legs, at first not wanting to be found, then not letting us go without the penalty of scratches and pain.

Topping and tailing the pithy stalks split our soft nails. My mother sat us down in front of the tennis on television with plastic tubs full of the collected berries. She joined us if Billie Jean King was playing on Centre Court at Wimbledon.

'Why do they say love all the time?'

We would ask this with a knowing smirk. Love was a daring word to utter in front of our mother.

'What has love got to do with hitting a ball over a net?'

'I thought love was kissing.'

We persisted when no answer was forthcoming until she insisted:

'Concentrate on your job.'

---

[56] J.R.R. Tolkien.

To conserve grass my father strip-grazed fields in the summer. This meant stringing an electric fence wire across the width of the pasture and moving the posts that held the wire about a metre twice a day exposing strips for the cows to feed on rather than giving them access to the whole field at once. Running at the heels of our father as he moved each rubber handled metal post, our wellies slapped against our bare legs as we darted and dodged to avoid accidentally touching the fence and getting a kick of electric current through our bodies. The fence gave a shock that my father seemed oblivious to and he would often tease us by brushing against our arms whilst holding the live wire with his other hand, but it was never enough to deter us from accompanying him.

'Anyone comin' to move the fence?'

'Yesss, meee,' was the chorus as we tumbled over the doorstep.

There was an unspoken joy in mingling with the animals, watching their quiet habits, knowing we nudged along in co-existence. We smelt the soft sticky cow dung, their sweet thick breath mixing with our own alongside the green scent that warm grass exudes when it is full of sunlight. We all had chlorophyll in our bones.

Recently, walking the dogs beside a thorn hedge, I notice the haws have swiftly replaced the blossom with tiny berries, about the size of a toddler's fingernail, standing proud on short firm stems. They are round, green and glossy. At their crown, the dying blossom has pealed back to leave a 'candle' with a wick where the flower once sat. These small hard beads will plump up red-ripe, coming into their own in autumn as an important part of the food chain for birds that winter in the dale. But in the syrupy heat of this late June day, they symbolise cyclical life; nature looking to the next season, to sustain the lives that will follow on. This is a lesson we must never forget or ignore.

Hawthorn is a pagan symbol of fertility and has connotations of illicit love and untamed desire. For some, including my grandmother, it was thought to invite illness and death if brought indoors, though there was a belief that the thorns protected a house from evil spirits and so wreaths would be made to hang on the outer side of external doors. Unlike the transience of our short lives, hawthorn bushes can survive for up to four hundred years. Their name is derived from the Old English term for hedgerows, a tribute to the way it dominates the centuries of boundaries planted into our landscape.

To achieve the full cycle of haymaking, without rain falling on the cut grass, was the most earnest aim of all farmers in the summer months. Mowing, wuffling (named after the equipment used),[57] windrowing, baling, stooking, leading in, stacking, were all to be managed within the parameters of the weather forecast. Good green hay gave nutritious fodder, whilst rain-soaked grass turned the bales musty and had little feed value when given to the animals in winter making my father wheeze as he scattered it into the hayracks.

A tender dawn unfurls over grass-swollen pastures; a morning dry with southerlies as you cut for hay. Noon air smells of memory, like a peony.

You catch sight of a hare, sit together for a while, watch the day slowly fading from green, instincts in tune, both understanding that all of this is borrowed.

There was a sense of optimism as the first grass of the season was cut. It was a physical process which needed both strength of mind and body. When, inevitably, the baler would break down mid-row, sweat would run down my father's forehead, as machinery and man pitched against each other. On his back, he wrenched the bones of metal into order before weather and engineering conspired to defeat the work ahead. There was a sense of immediacy, a race against the closing sky that taunted the last promise of daylight. Neighbours arrived before evening milking to help stook bales into 'sevens' ready for collection with the tractor and trailer.

Primary school over for the day, we acted out the Wild West amongst the bales. Native Americans ambushing cowboys, we carried cap-guns, loaded with a strip of tape that gave a loud crack and a puff of burnt matches when the trigger was pulled. Then we were lions prowling for prey and bomber pilots swooping to target the enemy until my mother strolled into the field, tea-filled enamel billy-can in hand, wicker basket over her arm. The men, one by one, drew to their ease, wiping dust-smeared foreheads, they settled with their backs against the tractor wheels or hay bales, chewing wisps of dried timothy grass, before the offer of egg and tomato sandwiches and warm buttery sultana tea-loaf. Although there were few words exchanged between the adults as they ate, companionship and support spoke in the silence.

We sat apart from the men, drinking juice before eagerly finishing the remnants of the picnic as they resumed their work. When we grew into our teens, we were given the job of driving the tractor whilst the men loaded the trailer with bales. After roping up there was the final rutted journey back to the farmstead

---

[57] Bamford Wuffler.

before dusk descended. Our reward was a rollercoaster ride on top of the load as it rocked the stony road home; the parcels of hay smelling of honey, filling our lungs, solace for achy-bone tiredness, hours of physical work complete.

My father cuts the lawn on a pendulum. I glimpse the young man, haymaking, windrowing years into years. He admires the planting of geraniums. I am in the fields breathing in the sweet-green afternoon. All days set to rhythm, like the hum that is sung by the baler. My memories belong to childhood, but my father's belong to a lifetime, fold the man into the field as decades gather in. Together, sitting on this neat mown grey-sky square, the toil of his day to remember, the young man who made the hay.

The gathering of winter fodder was a preoccupation in the summer months. Shortages of, and the price of hay, silage, barley, wheat and potatoes, higher in a wet year, were discussed over five bar gates with neighbours. Fearful of long cold winters, conversations invariably took a turn towards economics and the cost of survival:

'They're talkin' about interest rates havin' to go up again.'

A worried silence ensued.

'Inflation!'

'Bloody politicians.'

'They're all the same.'

'And petrol's goin' up again.'

'Four shillin' a gallon.'

'Aye.'

Most of our neighbours still dealt in 'old' money despite decimalisation[58] and had an intrinsic scepticism towards anything to do with change. The price of oil, and the fear of subsequent inflation, trade union strikes and the fracturing of relationships between the government and workers was destroying the known order of things. Successive general elections in the 1970s did little to stabilise the country. The introduction of a three-day working week was manifested in turbulence and disorder; society and culture were leaving behind the old ways.

'There's nothin' right about change for change's sake,' was a constant complaint.

---

[58] Decimalisation was introduced in February 1971 and it was widely feared that all prices would rise consequently. Four shillings would be the equivalent of £2.80 in 2020.

Resistance was embedded. The new world order was an unwelcome predator along Tunstall Road. But as I grew, I came home from school with ideas of my own:

'I don't want to leave school after my O levels. Maybe I'll do sixth form.'

'Girls don't need A levels. Nobody goes to university in our family.'

'You divvent need A levels to work in Woollies.[59] You'll be married before you're twenty,' my father added unhelpfully.

Neither prediction came true. I did go on to further my education, though university was a step too far for my parents and I finally studied for my degree as a mature student twenty years after leaving school.

§

As children, oblivious of wider world issues, summer was our golden time. The lambing finished; the lighter nights brought the start of the cricket season. We played 'tip it and run' in the drying green beside the farmhouse all day if enough friends and neighbours could be mustered. It was highly competitive.

'Everyone for themselves.'

This was established from the start and was the most important rule.

'If you hit the ball over the wall you're out.'

'An' if it goes into my veggie garden, you'll be fo' the high jump,' quipped my father.

When other families come over for Sunday lunch, a challenge at the crease preceded pudding. These were the heady days of Geoff Boycott, a Yorkshire batsman and county hero. My mother played cricket for Catterick in the local Ladies Cricket League, so my parents often practised after we were all in bed. My sister and I, lying side by side, listened as the leather ball tapped the willow, each parent taking their turn to bat then bowl in quiet order.

In our young teens the long school holiday was full of adventure. My mother would pack us a snack and a bottle of juice and we would set off on our bikes to wander the lanes that meandered through local villages. In the days before mobile phones, she would not know where we were until we returned for tea, but there was never any mention of being worried even if we were later home than expected.

---

[59] FW Woolworth's in Richmond.

Playing cricket in the drying green in our wellies. We played with my mother's full-sized bat from being not much taller than the blade and handle.

Although not venturing too far, this was a freedom we relished. The books we devoured at bedtime, *Famous Five*,[60] *Little Women*,[61] and *Anne of Green Gables*,[62] provided the backdrop to our explorations. Cousins came down from Newcastle and Northumberland, or over from Northallerton to stay for a few nights and seamlessly joined in with our games. Unless it was pouring with rain, we were swept out with the breakfast crumbs first thing on a morning:

'There's no such thing as boredom, so don't be coming back indoors complaining you've got nothing to do or I'll give you a job.'

This threat was sufficient to stimulate imaginations beyond the back door.

Marmalade was made at the beginning of the year when bitter Seville oranges were available at the greengrocers. But summer jam season was memorable for the cloying aroma that clung to our kitchen in the long hours of daylight. On jam days, the big brass pan that belonged to my great-grandmother was brought out to sit regally on the cooker hob. My mother bought strawberries

---

[60] Enid Blyton
[61] Louisa May Alcott.
[62] L.M. Montgomery.

and raspberries from a farm in Tunstall run by a pair of round and ruddy faced 'twins', who laughed their way through every conversation. Visiting their farm was like stepping back into the Edwardian era. Their stackyard was host to a scattering of rusting antiquated farm equipment: a horse-drawn flat-field roller, a hand-held seed fiddle, a cast iron turnip chopper powered by the manual turning of an axle. This machinery spoke of laborious and outdated farming practices, now lazing alongside stinging nettles, ground elder and broad-leaved docks. But memory recalls their yard smelt of sweet hay and ripe soft fruit dissolving into the backdrop of their buttermilk painted farmhouse.

Their kitchen was a functional rectangle room and retained the old black range with its open fire and old-fashioned high-backed wooden settle that snuggled in adjacent to the hearth, the wooden seat was dipped and bottom-worn from generations of family. Multi-coloured clippy mats[63] scattered haphazardly across the stone floor. Shiny custard-coloured wallpaper graced the walls, marked out in little squares patterned with blue delphiniums and pink roses. A large pine table exhaled with the weight of sweet, red berries ready for collection in cardboard baskets. The breeze through open windows made the curtains dance.

This old farmhouse exuded a charm and quaintness that had been stripped out of most houses by the 1970s. Their kitchen was a lament to the disappearing village farm and a way of doing things that celebrated a sensible and uncomplicated way of life; even then, it was a museum.

Strawberry breath so thick it sticks to walls, to skin, to cows that graze close by the snicket. Jam pan, copper and zinc, fruit and sugar, simmers mid-summer, an alchemy of adolescence, pulsing the solstice, bubbling over into the last exam, last sports day, last holiday before the swallow-wires of September speak of flight.

My father's vegetable patch nestled with angular neatness behind the lopsided garage in the lower stackyard, edged by fruit trees, rough ground and the bull-pen wall.

At bedtime, during the warmer light months, there was a comfort in knowing father was nearby, hoeing, weeding, planting and nurturing every corner of the land on which we lived. Potatoes were grown in the fields, but his garden was

---

[63] Rugs hand-made by women folk, from many equal sized strips of rags which were looped through hessian, so that their cut ends made a thick serviceable surface to the rug. Sometimes called proggy or hooky mats, after the equipment used to push the rags through the backing, they were a way of putting every scrap of old fabric to good use.

the domain of peas, carrots, beetroot, onions, beans, leeks, strawberries, rhubarb, and sweet pea flowers, which were a vegetable plot favourite with more than one local farmer; finely tilled soil with well-loved plants thriving in waves of neatness; a parenting.

Then surreptitiously August sneaks in on rowan trees, their clusters of red berries ringing out the beginnings of farewell to summer. The sycamore and ash turn their leaves towards the autumn air. Evenings start to give way to dusk with noticeable speed. Outdoor play is cut short; warm days cool quickly. Back-end creeps into conversations.

The return to school after summer hailed harvest and blackberry picking. Nimble fingers dived into bushes to gather these gems of the hedgerows that teased with their swollen juiciness. My mother encouraged us to take a bowl and pick the fruit she needed to make jellies, jams, crumbles and pies for winter puddings. We preferred the spontaneity of stealing and eating them straight from the briars that wove their way through field maple, elder and holly hedging.

As stained lips betray, we crack our fists in pursuit of one last berry from a corner of summer.

Folklore claims that when the devil was kicked out of heaven, he fell into a bramble bush and in revenge cursed any berries left unpicked after 29th September, Old Michaelmas Day, or Devil Spit Day. In truth, fruit left so late in the season is usually mouldy and fly blown and cannot be eaten.

Time begins to bronze, bruises the aging year. But time cares not where the apples fall, where the thistle seeds stray, if the sap now drains and the cocksfoot grass wilts. Time can never belong, is never past or what is to come; even September is just a name.

Conkers were a late September pastime and much looked forward to. We sat them on the hearth beside the fire to dry and harden, then pierced their mahogany shells with a screwdriver or metal skewer, threading string through and knotting it in readiness for conker matches with friends. To have a sixer or above was a great achievement.[64]

---

[64] A conker that had won six rounds or matches by destroying the competitor's conker whilst remaining intact.

Harvest festival meant the gathering of locally grown produce to decorate the Church window ledges and altar. All the children brought along home grown produce to this annual event attended by the whole school. Cabbages, potatoes, cauliflowers, chrysanthemum, even sheafs of barley, were gifted. Today, in contrast, non-perishables are preferred, tins of tropical fruit in syrup, packets of digestive biscuits and jars of manufactured pickle are considered more practical offerings to distribute after the service.

The main Church annual harvest service would follow the school's celebration. Many who lived in rural outposts joined the congregation of village folk, filling St Anne's with thanks for another year of bounty. Farmers, who never attended a service during the year would put on their best and more than likely only suit to come and give thanks. Wives and children accompanied the menfolk, although for them the Church was less of an enigma, attending regularly on Sundays throughout the year. However, recognising the safe garnering of field crops was an important event on the calendar of our small community of farms. Harvest hymns were uplifting and a popular choice at the funerals of farming friends and relatives.

After the formalities of the service a supper was held in the village hall where some of the produce would be auctioned off, the rest was given to the elderly and needy of the parish.

Historically, farming and the Church littered the year with such occasions, many inherited from pre-Christian customs. Rogation days[65] were marked with the walking of parish boundaries and the blessing the fields that fell within them. This stemmed from ancient beliefs that in doing so crops would be protected from disease.

Religious thanksgiving and witchery often run side-by-side in rural communities, autumn being the season of mists, ghouls and superstition. Every deed that helped towards good fortune and kept bad omens at bay was never a wasted action. Whilst farmers may have had little spare money themselves, back end[66] was abundant with natural riches that were embraced as gifts.

If we were lucky late August and September brought mushrooms to our fields.

'Look for mushrooms in an unploughed field that used to have horses in it,' my grandmother advised.

---

[65] Rogation is derived from the Latin 'to ask'. Linked to Easter and Ascension Day the idea of rogation was borrowed from pagan customs.
[66] A colloquial term for autumn.

Coming in from morning milking my father would deposit cushions of dark-gilled fungi on the draining board.

'Mushrooms for breakfast, get the toast on.'

One season the fields floated on clouds of the smooth creamy caps. Neighbours were invited to help themselves and still the mushrooms returned each morning. In folklore an abundance of mushrooms predicts a snowy winter, on our land it meant soups and quiches for dinner.

Do you remember early autumn evenings? The murmuration of starlings swelling and swooping as we strolled the coffin route home? When you wore my hand in your pocket? When you told me the stories of how the moon heals our darkest hours? Where the mushrooms hide?

On our farm potatoes were a precious cash crop and not to be squandered. Like many with limited land we only grew a couple of acres for our own consumption and to sell at the farm gate over the winter months. Our yield did not warrant layout on expensive machinery and so my siblings and I were the workforce. October school holidays were filled with the necessary employment. My father spun the potatoes out of the earth with his little grey Fergie linked up to an old-fashioned mechanical spinner sporting a wheel of hooked arms. Row by row we stooped to fill our buckets with the newly exposed potatoes, their bodies like new-born, pale and soft skinned, surprised to be lifted so brutally from their womb of soil. The buckets were emptied into re-used cattle feed bags and loaded onto the trailer to take back to the farm at the end of the day.

We were thankful for the declining daylight of late October afternoons that helped shorten the hours of this back-breaking task. The crop was emptied in the Dutch barn and pied with straw and hessian sacks to protect the contents from frosts. During the winter, the pie was opened once a week and the potatoes sorted into batches: small ones were kept and planted as sets in the spring, the larger potatoes weighed, ready for selling, and any that were rotten, taken out before they spread their disease to others.

I was in my mid-teens when I took a holiday job picking potatoes with a large arable farmer near Ripon. Our gang of youngsters were collected early in the morning by one of the empty lorries used for transporting potatoes to the McCain factory near Scarborough. We heaved ourselves up, spilling over the steep sides, rolling to the bottom of the large metal trailer behind the cab. With a tarpaulin cover, we sat in darkness, rumbled and tossed like a chip in a fryer for twenty miles down to the fields where we worked all day.

Once we arrived, picking was achingly intense. We formed two lines and grubbed up and down the rows tipping the contents of our filled plastic baskets into the trailer that followed in-between each gang up the field. Elevenses, or *'llowance*,[67] as many elders called it, was the first stop of the day. The boys who drove the tractors would sing bawdy rugby songs and tell blue jokes to their captive audience, raucous laughter and sweet tea brought relief from our labours. After a fifteen-minute break we continued until lunchtime when we ate our bait,[68] finally finishing an hour after our short three o'clock break. We were paid cash at the end of each day as we alighted from the lorry that dropped us back off near home. This was the first time I had ever earned and owned a twenty-pound note. But, I was soon parted from it to become the proud owner of a brown bomber jacket, like one worn by Suzy Quattro, which fooled me into thinking it made me look just like her.

November would often fend off winter by imposing dark, mild downcast days filled with mud and murk. Pheasants and robins shared our slide into decreasing daylight with their sudden visibility against the bones of the land.

Hedgerows relinquish frost-pinched leaves: crab apple, hazel, beech-rust kernels, strands of sloe berries dark as coal, knotted into scaly twigs, talons like crow's feet. Sapless earth is shedding its skin, exposing the dale. We laze amongst late scabious, devil bitten, dry to husk, as the swell of decay dresses for northerlies.

Where distance folds into distance, fells run barefoot, their footprints merging with peat. The pouring moor is soft and grim. Clouds brood, moan their iced breath where the tame dale ends and juniper trees crouch. Swaledale is veiled in the cinnamon of winter.[69]

Silent snowfall brought magic, casting a blue-white hue over the fields. Drifts regularly levelled with the tops of walls and filled the farm lane meaning the milk lorry could not make it up the track to pick up the churns. Sheep were to dig free from frozen tombs; 'snowed in' was no exaggeration. The world came to a halt and for a few hours the farm became prey to polar air; an island in an arctic sea.

---

[67] Allowance was the term used for the permitted break workers were given by their employers.
[68] A working packed lunch usually of sandwiches or cheese.
[69] Inspired by reading the work of Ella Pontefract & Marie Hartley, 1934, *Swaledale*, London: J.M. Dent & Sons Ltd.

Significant snowfall brought disruption in the form of big drifts. 1947 and 1963 were the notable years that broke records. Here, it is the winter of 78/79.

Ambushed, the farmhouse awakens to snow sliding over the doorstep, creeping up the windowpanes, shutting us inside. It steals the map of the fields, hiding their contours from us. The glacial air clears our nostrils, fills our lungs with an aura that cleanses our bodies, making us light-headed and ungrounded, eager to loose ourselves in the frenzy of white.

I remember evenings when I would run through the gate next to the drying green as the bloom of a full moon lit the silken field luminous: ethereal. I easily wintered into this landscape, revelled in the fragility etched by the ice on puddles, in the snap of stiff coats worn by last season's leaves.

Tonight, I follow Taurus, Canis Major, Cygnus, tread carefully with Perseus, wear their constellations under my feet, gather their ice into my fingers, hold the oldest dust on earth.

'There'll be more snow before we know it. The old snow is still in the hedgebacks.'
Father's folklore was once more prophesying the weather, yet so often this adage rings true.

Looking back, I picture the Christmas days of childhood, glazed in fresh snow or bitter hoar frosts, though how frequently this really was the case is debatable.

December was not a time for sentimentality on the farm; work did not stop for Christmas. In fact, the week preceding it was more memorable than the festivities themselves. To provide another strand of income, my father reared poultry for the Christmas dinner table. The kitchen, back-yard and small dairy attached to the porch were used in preparing and storing the dressed birds before they were sold. The whole house smelt brutal.

In the week before Christmas came the bloodbath. When others hung baubles, we hung the necks of chickens. The back kitchen, a butcher's shop brimming with death and the purr of machine that stripped bare the feathers, pulled without mercy from lifeless flesh, our breath cut sharp on the metallic stench of innards: gizzard, liver, neck, packed back into each wrenched empty carcass. Bodies laid out in a makeshift morgue.

After the last of the oven-ready birds had been delivered, Christmas Eve was upon us. It was then we would dress the living room in paper chains from corner to corner, the tree was brought inside, and anticipation became fervent.

We scrub the raw meat from our hands until the house, freed of slaughter, is given back to us. These same hands, now warmed by pine and spices, wrap gifts in bright tissue, hang tinsel and lights on the tree. Nearby, the hum of the wireless spills carols and IRA murders into our living room. Sometimes, an occasional white feather finds its way onto the sofa; a calling-card from the dead.

On Christmas Day cows had to be milked, and stock fed before we opened our presents from Santa. After lunch, and the Queen's speech, my father rose from his chair and returned to the farmyard. My sister, brother and I then made our way across the fields to pay a call on Tommy and his wife. The community of small farms in which we lived was a family with which to share special events.

New Year's Eve, and an unusually warm south-westerly rages. We walk, huddled down, using the protection of drystone walls like Swaledale sheep, listen to the rant of the storm ripping its way through the brittle moorland, stripping the land of its breath.

'I've just seen a man with as many noses as there are days left this year.'
My grandmother teased with this statement on the last day of the year.
'What!'
'Where?'
'When?'
'Can I see?'
Of course, every New Year's Eve we believed her until we were all old enough to work it out for ourselves.

Our farming year was forever prone to pitfalls: disease, drought and floods, cheap imports, a downfall in prices, machinery breakdowns. These were just some of the day-to-day setbacks that would hinder or defeat. So, as the year turned, we protected ourselves with customs and habits called upon to allay bad luck. One such tradition was first footing.

A remnant of coal lies twelve months in the darkness of the sideboard drawer, exiled in an overcoat of long forgotten news, until the five-to-midnight rummage. Her fossilised hands, worn in carbon dust, passes the nugget to a dark stranger. In night air, smoky with the dying embers of the year, his first footing brings hopes of good fortune over her threshold. Reassured, she wraps the coal back into yesterday's stories. Weather, weddings and obituaries, as the sediment of her own years compact one on one on one.

BIRTH AND DEATH
'when the spaces along the road between here and there are all used up, that's it'[70]

Death shimmered on the surface of the farm. New life and the dying were our constant companions. We had a pragmatic acceptance of death. It was indiscriminate, sometimes emotional, but always matter of fact. Cows died giving birth, new-born calves died more frequently from many varied causes. With clover-lush grass came the fear of bloat in young cattle.[71] Sheep died just because they could. A beloved farm dog was run over and killed by the milk man. Kittens were often drowned before their eyes opened. One cat knew to give birth off the farm, so she hid across the fields in a redundant cow-byre, or a neighbour's haystack. When her offspring's eyes opened, she carried them home into our barn, their tiny bodies swinging from her mouth by the back of their necks. Her sense of maternal protection knew when they were old enough to be out of danger from harm.

On chilly winter evenings, before bedtime we huddled around the fire in our pyjamas, knees tucked up like snails in shells to protect us from the elements within the house. Doors rattled themselves free during a gale, towels hugged windowsills in downpours to catch the rainwater that found its way indoors, the open kitchen window was an extractor fan no matter what the external temperature.

During lambing time in late March, we shared the fireside with the frailest lambs; often this warmth was the difference between death and survival. My father would bring the seriously unwell inside wrapped in an old flannelette sheet. He rubbed their skinny bodies to warm them, lying them down beside the hearth in hope of stirring life. These little blue faced Leicester lambs sported legs like new-born foals, too long for them to manage with ease. Their bodies were see-through, a coat of skin-pink with a thin covering of short cream curls. Their faces were endearing, no matter their state of health; ears to grow into, and large dewy eyes. We nestled up close to them stroking their unflinching bodies willing them to lift their heads, but they were indifferent to their surroundings. Tempting these new lambs not to die centred us into a respect for all life.

---

[70] Galway Kinnell, *The Road Between Here and There*.
[71] An accumulation of gas in the stomach that can kill livestock.

When stock was sick my father often put his faith in a healing man. Mr Dutton was an animal doctor who had learned his trade with a combination of science and instinct and was well respected for his knowledge. There were times when he could not provide a cure, and he said so; other occasions when the local vet failed, he succeeded. He was an alchemist, a sage; a figure from the past who holds few equivalents today. Vitally important to a farmer, he was a cheaper alternative than a visit from the vet.

Vets were male, that is until the ground-breaking day that sent shockwaves through the community when a local veterinary practice appointed a newly qualified woman.

Sarah was a match for all the animals she encountered. When she first arrived, there were mutterings about a female calving cows and how would it be possible for a woman to pitch her weight against a bull or a horse? But she was a pioneer and here to challenge the scathing minds of farming men and their womenfolk.

'She's only a young lass. Who heard the likes?' muttered the elders entrenched in the rigidity of the right and wrong of how things had to be done, but most importantly, there to condemn if things were not done right.

'Women vets, what next? I've nivver heard the likes.'

'It nivver 'apppened in my day.'

'She needs a husband and a few bairns then there'll be no time for veterinarying.'

But Sarah was a role model to the young of both sexes.

Unlike Sarah, Mr Dutton rarely came out to the farms, instead we had to drive up to his house in Wensleydale to pick up the medicines he had concocted himself. This was another outing with my father we rarely wanted to miss. Mr Dutton lived in a wooden facia boarded bungalow, larger, but not dissimilar to the one in our drying green. This alone made him fascinating.

The medicine man was tall, grey haired and unassuming. His summer garden lined a well-trodden flagged path to his front door. It was neatly rowed with regimented vegetables in straight lines saluting spires of purple and yellow lupins, pastel pink phlox and fragrant strands of honeysuckle trained over a wooden arch. It was an orchestrated palette of scent and colour; the antithesis of the untamed and rusted uplands that rampaged over the horizons he looked out on to at the back of his property. Such a garden, full of growth and healthy plants, seemed incompatible with a man who dealt with despair and last-hope remedies.

Luck plays a great part in farming. On the few occasions we left the farm with a relief milker for a few days away on the Yorkshire coast at Scarborough or Filey, invariably an animal died. Worst of all was when it happened to a cow. The loss was not only financial, but it unexpectedly broke a lineage that linked far back into the body of the herd. Each death left a trace that mapped with significance over our lives too.

'She was out of Ricdon Queenie 11th.'[72]

My father held all this information in his head.

'Only two calvings. First one was a heifer then a bull last year, the heifer is out in the Well field now.'

'She was a good milker. I'll miss her.'

Occasionally birth asserted supremacy. One cow had two sets of triplets in under twelve months: almost unheard of. All six calves survived.

Mothering. My sister and I feed hungry Mule lambs. This was not a long job; despite their size, they would devour this bottle in a few minutes. Sometimes if a ewe had lost her lambs during birth when she came into her milk my father would try to encourage her to adopt an orphaned lamb. Her dead lamb would be skinned and the pelt tied onto the adoptee in the hope the smell would transfer onto the body of the live lamb and the ewe would take to it.

---

[72] Ricdon was an amalgamation of my father's last name, Richardson, and my mother's birth name, Donald. The prefix of the herd was registered with the British Friesian Society.

Pet lambs were a delight for us, if not my father. A lamb might be orphaned or a weaker lamb taken from a ewe with triplets and hand-fed to survive. Ewes only have two teats, this is a basic design fault on an animal that can produce three or, occasionally, four offspring at once. Nurturing new-born lambs, before they decided to die, might involve giving them stints under a hot lamp in a make-shift straw-bale pen and regular feeds of formula milk from a bottle topped with a black teat. For a while, feeding the lambs was a novelty until Wacky Races or Crackerjack[73] called us to the television, or sometimes when the cold bit our fingers too much, we would happily abandon the job to our mother.

Once, at the beginning of an art lesson in primary school, the teacher announced:

'We have a special visitor today.'

'Is it the inspector miss?'

'No. It's a baby.'

The classroom murmurs swelled and small wooden chairs shuffled with anticipation.

'Be quiet now. You will scare it with your chatter. Sssh and I will invite them in.'

'Who is it miss?'

My mother walked into the classroom with one of our pet lambs in her arms.

I silently thanked her for the kudos it gave me, suddenly awash with importance and knowledge beyond that of my peers.

'I saw this one being born.'

I had scant care for the truth and continued to impart my expertise to those who would listen.

'It's a gimmer.'

'That's a girl sheep.'

Afterwards, I was teased with some alternative words to 'Mary had a little lamb', but my siblings and I were never short of friends who wanted to spend a day with us on the farm at weekends, especially when pet lambs were to be fed.

---

[73] Wacky Races was an American animated series first released in 1968; Crackerjack was a British TV show which began in 1955.

Occasionally a ewe threw out a black lamb unfit for the pedigree line of my father's Bluefaced Leicesters.[74] Sadly, whether a gimmer or a tup, when grown and fattened it was destined for our deep freeze. The day the rubber-aproned butcher arrived in the yard was accompanied by the dread of chasing the unfortunate animal around the field and bringing it in to the old pig-hole building to meet its fate.

'We'll enjoy this one, nice bit of meat.'

My father would make comments whilst kneading the haunches of the poor sheep. As the animal gasped with fear, the pale amber eyes seemed to draw towards my own. I could see the terror darting behind the depths of their marbled sheen. The desire to eat meat drained away in moments such as these.

Geld[75] cows and young bullocks, even the bantams that strutted the stackyard with all the confidence of their larger contemporary, the white Leghorn cockerel, were all destined for the pot eventually. The killing of a sheep, and subsequent return of the butcher to divide the carcase into manageable joints was marked by the smell of raw meat being transported into the house in our old pink plastic baby bath; life continually demonstrating its cyclical nature.

Sex education had long been completed before we sat in the biology lab in the first year at secondary school giggling our way through the teacher's discomfort and diagrams. There was never a time in our growing that the process of reproduction was not laid before us with the serving of cows, either by the bull or through a visit from the AI man bringing the thin sliver of a semen rod which disappeared, along with his hand and half his arm, into the cow's vagina.[76]

Conception and birth were everyday occurrences. Watching a calf slip from its mother in a rush of blood and afterbirth held a passing fascination if we happened to be around the calving house. A bantam hen sitting on her eggs was an event that was so commonplace it went unnoticed. Hatched chicks were an arresting sight, but as soon as their scruffy, half-feather, half-down, bodies

---

[74] Bluefaced Leicester sheep are a longwool breed coming originally, in the 18th century, from Dishley in Leicestershire, and valued for their fine fleece and milk yield. When they are crossbred with upland ewes, such as Swaledale, Cheviot or Scottish Blackface, they produce a sheep known as a north country mule. The advantage of crossbreeding is to promote more economic options for upland farmers, for example, in rearing lambs for the meat market. Pure-bred upland ewes are natural mothers and provide the core of a flock. A nicely configured Bluefaced Leicester tup to run with his own flock, or to sell to use for crossing, was the constant drive behind my father's breeding programme. Today, an exceptional young Bluefaced Leicester tup can bring into the tens of thousands at auction.

[75] A barren cow beyond her best breeding years.

[76] Artificial insemination.

reached gangly teenage years, they seemed to vanish into the backdrop of the yard, to become just another banty. The rudiments of life were sown into us from being very young, and if we had not quickly joined the dots in the line to copulation for ourselves, then the boys on the farm across the road had the necessary graphic vocabulary to hand.

Both my sister and brother were born in my parent's bedroom. I cannot remember being aware of the expected deliveries, only vague recollections of both days when the district nurse, a neighbour's wife and my father, filled the house with their hushed tones as my mother took to her bed. When my sister was born, I can recall being told to ride my tricycle up and down the garden path in a bid to keep me occupied and out of the way, but I never queried from what I was being kept.

Soon after each delivery my father descended the stairs to take my hand and lead me back up to meet my new-born sibling. By this time my mother was sat up in bed with the baby swaddled so tight to her I could only see a nose from my tiptoes.

Then the memory fades, as did my interest. I had an imaginary friend called Donder and spent my pre-school years quite happily playing alone with them. Donder remained my companion until I started school and then disappeared without another word. But not before the patience of my mother had been tried when I would insist on a place being set for them at the table at mealtimes, and cried if she shut the door before Donder had been able to get into the car.

Seeing my mother with a baby was no more remarkable to me than every cow or ewe I had witnessed with their young. The day after each event my grandmother arrived to stay for a period. There is no memory of disruption to everyday life. Early childhood was sheltered and otherwise uneventful.

§

On a walk in Cotterdale, we pass through a farmyard and are confronted by the realities of birth and death in the form of two wire cages: one containing two carrion crows, the other a vocal magpie. These winged vermin can peck the eyes out of vulnerable new-born lambs given the chance. They are also known to attack the ewes as they are giving birth. There are many more predators, such as foxes, lying in wait for the weak. Catching and caging these birds represents a desperate attempt to protect valuable stock. Once the lambs are older and strong enough to run, they can look after themselves. But the birds must feed their young too. The battle between nature and farming is as old as the cultivated land on which we stand.

Pheasant shooting spans from the 1st October through to 31st January. My father never owned a shotgun and had no interest in doing so, unlike many farmers. This meant neighbours came shooting on our land. As a way of saying thank you they would leave a brace or two of pheasants behind. The limp-necked birds, too beautiful to die, were tied together with string around their necks and hung on the inside of the small dairy door just off the house porch, a room used for egg packing and storing animal medicines. Their presence was confirmed with a slap against the back of this door as it is opened and closed even when old winter work coats hid them. The sound was a dull requiem without colour or charm.

In contrast, their lifeless bodies were still vibrant in death; vivid red wattles, necks of bottle green and electric blue with a white vicar's collar and dappled rich coppery bodies extending elegantly into long tails. They hung there for days as the meat aged to give flavour before my mother took them down and with bucket in hand, ploated[77] and drew the innards, preparing them for the pot. From an early age I could not equate food with these majestic creatures that filled our clumps of woodland with their incongruous creaky-door-call when we surprised them. Finding small, lead-shot pellets in their cooked flesh exacerbated my distaste for eating the birds and animals we shared the land with.

Red grouse inhabit the uplands of Swaledale. When disturbed the male grouse shouts, 'getbackgetbackgetback' as he scuttles into flight. This command echoes across open skies; a voice that reminds us that in the natural order of things man is the predator.

Black grouse are rarer than their red counterparts. If you are lucky, and know where you will find them, during April and May, the males, or blackcocks, partake in a ritual called lekking.[78] Early in the morning they gather, fanning their white under-tail out against the body's darker feathers, sparring with other males, ten or more, to gain territory and win females, known as greyhens.

Another bird with a distinctive cry like the black grouse is the snipe. The rhythmic vibrating huuuw-huuuw-huuuw that reverberates over the upland above Downholme on a spring dawn feels primeval. This is not a call, but a drumming that is produced from the wings of the male snipe as he dives

---

[77] To pluck the feathers off the bird.
[78] Lek is the Old Norse word for play.

through the air after a circling display of courtship. It is ritualistic, as if an ancient dance is resurfacing through the energies of this small, shy, wading bird.

By early March, the curlew's melancholic cry should be resounding high above the moor. So often the first sighting of the season is a solitary curlew; gliding into spring with a voice that yearns for the lost curlews that no longer return to grace this wild place. Hearing their music in early spring is a quasi-religious experience. Their trail of notes are elevating yet have an eery quality. These wistful, independent birds occupy a liminal space, fill the bleak, long-wintering uplands with the promise of awakening:

Over the cattle grid, the horizon widens and hours become a prairie as a sudden mournful cry untethers March. His wild echo arcs the moor, opens us up to the sky. We have held our breath all winter for this joy, ripple with his insistent prayer, imagine a thousand sorrows in one song.

Sadly, we have destroyed many of the curlew's natural breeding grounds. Today's numbers are a fraction of those of the past. Their decline is attributed to intensive farming and the diminution of their natural habitat. The un-wilding of traditional moorland has had far reaching effects. Changes in agriculture means edges of many uplands are drained and brought into useable land, to the determent of all birds who choose to breed on these wide expanses. So often ground-nesting birds have their offspring mown down by grass-cutters employed to collect early crops of silage, whereas hay-time traditionally came later when chicks had fledged.[79] Also, there is now indisputable evidence climate warming has a bearing on the invertebrate population of moors and bogs, impacting on food available for our migrating birds that fly in for the summer.

In recent years, the purposeful control of predators such as foxes and stoats, known to steal eggs and chicks, has had an influence on helping the curlew population. Now, some of the grouse shooting estates in the area are actively working to help boost the numbers of birds under threat, taking on their protection whilst simultaneously intensely managing the rearing of grouse.[80]

---

[79] A large modern tractor, with air-con cabs and surround sound systems, means the driver is often cocooned, oblivious to the wildlife under his wheels. Their predecessors, smaller cabless tractors, enabled the farmers to easily spot nests and cut around them when necessary.
[80] This is not without controversy.

The northern dales provide some of the last nesting sites in England for waders, thanks to managed environmental projects. But if curlews are to continue to return to these grounds they need a huge investment of knowledge, time and empathy if anything near their historical numbers is to be attained in the future.

In Wensleydale, a Curlew Safari will occasionally be offered to the public in early summer. It gives brief, controlled access to conservation areas where breeding programmes are being run. One June morning a small group of us set off in an assortment of land-rovers, along with the gamekeepers as our guides.

'Today, we'll hopefully see lapwing, snipe, redshank, woodcock and the highlight of course, curlews.'

We drive up a narrow, pitted moorland track at an angle that defies gravity. The gamekeeper suddenly stops the vehicle and turns to look across to the bank to which we are parallel.

'See over there.'

'Those little sparrow-like birds with a black line across their cheeks and blush chests.'

'Watch as they flit in and out of the holes in the soil.'

'They're little white arses: wheatears.'[81]

As we emerge onto heath and heather a curlew rises above us wailing a distracting cry to protect the location of the nest on which its partner sits; a job that both parents share in turn. As the vehicle stops, we all take up our binoculars.

'Look, there's a pair. See them gliding, she's up as well now. You can tell because she's larger than him, and the curve of her bill is more pronounced.'

'Curlews have different flight calls depending on whether they are agitated and protecting chicks, or just communicating with each other. They can make a right commotion if they want to.'

'Listen to that alarm call. They're very territorial.'

'We'll get out of their way so they'll come back down to the nest.'

'Look they're heading back to the flat grassland on top. See. I think the nest must be right the way over.'

We move on and he chats as he drives us along a stony track maintained for the grouse shooters.

---

[81] Wheatears sport a white rump. Their name derives from Old English.

'We used to think that the curlews on these uplands came from Russian broods. But by ringing the chicks we now know that these birds return to the same place they were hatched to lay their eggs.'

'The success rate in breeding the young chicks is still not as high as we would like. But, after nesting time we will bring cattle up onto these tops to graze. This helps with maintaining the density of grass and the breeding of insects to aid next spring's young.'

'Rearing double broods was once common, now they're mostly single due to the environment not being able to sustain more than one clutch of eggs per season.'

In listening to their planned management, it strikes me that our ancestors would be astounded how the human world has become so lax in laying foundations for the future, forward planning is a skill we have neglected too long.

Having reached the summit of the moor, we train our binoculars on the heather carpet and blanket bogs that sweep into a swathe of undulating horizons. Suddenly the gamekeeper has spied movement.

'See the large clump of common rush straight ahead beside the brownish peaty ground. To the right, there she is, look the chicks are following and the last one is trailing a couple of yards behind.'

'They like the wet places so they have a source of food nearby for the chicks. Things like spiders and beetles that live on the surface of the ground.'

Fragile fluffs of yellowy buff chitter behind their parents on long spindly grey legs supported by feet they will eventually grow into. Despite the lack of proportion, they move with grace in and out of the moss and ling.

'You'll notice the beak on the young ones hasn't got a curve yet. That'll come as they grow.'

'These chicks will fledge in July at about six weeks old and make their way with the rest of the flock to winter on the estuaries across country; coastal areas like Morecambe Bay.'

'With a bit of luck, some of them you see today will live to migrate in and out for the next twenty years or more.'

'In the past they used to think that hearing a curlew wailing after dark was a bad omen. That they were releasing the spirits of the dead. Yet their daytime bubbling sounds are made in courtship, a sign of hope.'

'Others saw them as a symbol of the loss and pain of parenting and associated them with the haunted cries of young children that had passed.'

'Another myth is that they steal the souls of those that are about to die...So, better keep your wits about you while you're up here.'

Further along the moor we come across a couple from a university study group carefully netting the curlew chicks then one-by-one tagging their legs with several rings; the coloured circlets sit away from the small body to allow room for growth. They explain this scheme is to monitor the birds migrating and breeding habits and be able to track them over several years to compile information that will further help the species survive.

With a final check on the rings the chicks are returned to their nests. Through the entire process the adult curlews have been screeching their alarm at the interference, circling above us in shrill repetitious notes.

'The young won't be abandoned will they because you've handled them?'

One of our party voices all our concern.

'No, we are careful and work swiftly, get them back to their parents in a few minutes.'

As the curlew chicks set out on their precarious path into adulthood, our group ripples with the exhilaration of being able to observe these vulnerable birds, even from a distance. The sobering prospect that future generations may lose the sound and sight of their wistful energy is never far from our thoughts. As conservationists are doing battle on the moorlands of these northern dales, we can only hope enough can be done in the time we have left to save these fabled birds.

We must help to manage the future with the care our forebears managed their legacy. We forget the diligence of those who came before us at our peril. Using farming methods now considered out-dated, our ancestors walked in step with the seasons and the land.

Modern farming practices - including ripping out hedgerows, the early cutting of grass for hay and silage, the use of chemicals to curtail disease and enhance productivity - all contribute to a wilful dismantling of the ecosystem. Had the custodians of the past not lived with a connection to the landscape and respect for those who would come after, our own voices would be echoes fading into obscurity.

We must read the land and observe what nature tells us. But in doing so never forget the natural world is without benevolence. Nature is its own organism with its own will.

No-one wants to regress in animal husbandry and crop production. We cannot go back to the old ways of doing things. Nature is continually one step in front of us. Too often we employ passive eyes, see the pastoral, the idyll; the past is not about sentimentality, it is a tool at our disposal to help us move forward. We should cherry-pick the wisdom of our ancestors and listen to what nature has been teaching us for centuries; what are best practices, what is damaging.

Re-wilding dominates our current discourse on the reintroduction of species back into their natural habitats. In my garden I have kept a sizeable chunk of land free from cultivation over several years, allowing it to manage itself. Year by year the bramble wickens,[82] with long, arching, thorny stems, quickly multiply and root themselves over and over into thickets. Yet these plants do not yield the juicy fruit that birds and small mammals feed on. At best they appear to tie themselves around every plant, strangling and suffocating many. This patch of garden is becoming a monoculture, hostile enough to keep me from attempting to re-introduce other plants. Yes, it will support a limited biodiversity of insects and small mammals, but no new bird species have ventured into the area; butterflies, bees, wildflowers and rabbits have not returned.[83]

Through my small and amateur experiment, I realise that there is a natural chain to be nurtured between two extremes and so I must de-wild until a balance is created. The area needs an essence of management to run wild and achieve the best outcome, which is the interdependency of as many species as possible. But if I intervene, am I manipulating the environment?

The destruction of so many natural habitats is at a precarious crossroads. Humans and nature are instilled with the same force of procreation. But, whatever our courses of action, nature will adapt and survive; however much it is depleted and decimated it will retain a presence in some form.

It is not the world we destroy; it is ourselves.

---

[82] A colloquial word we used word for bramble runners.
[83] I realise that this is all equated with scale.

GROWING UP
'I stand neither in the wilderness nor fairyland'[84]

My parents farmed with an abiding respect for our home. Their template traced over the shape of me as I grew through childhood. We lived on the land and in the land. Our first lessons came from the natural world. From swifts that glued their nests to the house eaves after long flights north from Africa, only to rebuild them repeatedly if heavy rain washed them away. We watched with awe as communities of swifts helped each other in this task. Listened to squabbles of seagulls that instinctively travel inland to scour damp, newly ploughed soil for food. Shivered in bitter winds blown in from the Arctic to stunt spring. All are signs and certainties, teaching us sensitivity to the seasons and a sensibility for our environment.

Beside the old quarry on our land, a vixen guides her young up from the belly of their underground home, encouraging them to play in the last warmth on a summer's evening. The cubs remind us of ourselves. Their sense of fun, cavorting against the ruby sky at the north-western edges of a sunset, bring our games to a halt. My father spies them first, their frisky young bodies relishing the freedom from a dark constricted den, the mother continually watchful for danger.

The freedom of wild animals and birds was seductive to my youthful imagination. Rules and restrictions, both at home and with homework, were frustrating, even more so when reaching secondary school.

'I want to be a sparrow.'

I announce this one evening as I listen to their spritely chatter ricocheting off the stackyard walls.

'A spuggy.'[85]

My brother is incredulous:

'You'd only get yourself shot.'

I feel indignant.

'No, I wouldn't. I would make sure I fly too fast for anyone to shoot me.'

Joseph's son, next door, had an air rifle and used these nimble, brown-bodied birds as target practice. For me though, the joy of being able to fly far

---

[84] Kathleen Jamie, *The Wishing Tree*.
[85] A colloquial name for a sparrow.

outweighed the perils of his pellets. The thought of being permanently grounded was not an option; flight was often on my mind.

The circumference of familiarity we lived in held us tight into a large surrogate family. But from our land, positioned on top of Prospect Hill, the compass spun in all directions, tempting us towards new adventures.

My parents pointed out when we crossed the east-west watershed on the high ground of Swaledale. They showed us where streams nestled into the ribs of the Pennines; where three old counties met, Westmorland, County Durham and the North Riding of Yorkshire, near Tan Hill Inn, the highest pub in England. This inn has survived at the top of the dale for so long, highwayman Dick Turpin is rumoured to have laid low here from the law in the 18th century.[86] Stories such as this seeded temptation to follow unknown tracks. As a teenager, I was Jack with a handful of beans and dreams of climbing a beanstalk to other places.

In a field one hundred and fifty metres from the farmstead, an aged hollow ash tree provided a shelter for me to ease my youthful body into. Under the cover of darkness, it offered my young mind the privacy of a place to contemplate, to create stories and poems: time to make sense of growing up. Crouched within the womb of wood, the tree nurtured me. There was no roof to this sanctuary. It opened to the stars and the moon like an observatory. Here, sitting underneath infinity, all things seemed possible. The dying tree spoke of cyclical life. It was my teacher.

In this secret space I could transform into whoever I wanted to be, a character from a book, a field mouse, a pop star. It allowed me to slip away from the practicalities of everyday. This was a haven, a place to harvest the best imaginings of my daydreams. From this hideaway I was a distant observer of the farms and houses that surrounded me. I sensed the happenings, the comings and goings, pans on the stoves, logs sparking on open fires, the menfolk foddering up, flushing out the dairy at the end of milking, cats at their heels winding their supple bodies around muck-clagged wellingtons.

§

We built dens extensively; just below the rafters of the hay shed was a favourite. The small gap where the top of the haystack sweated out it's heat

---

[86] Dick Turpin was infamous for highway robbery. He was hanged for theft in 1739.

under the wooden eaves and corrugated iron roof was a sauna. But this did not deter the endless fantasies of our play that expelled further hot air into the atmosphere. Billy-band was tied to joists so we could swing between the stacks Tarzan-like across pools of crocodiles, falling into the soft remnants of broken bales left from previous years, we screamed with the fear we might be eaten up:

'Jump further, higher.'

'You've got to get across the lagoon,' squealed our rescuers, the children from neighbouring farms.

'I will not be happy if you break good bales up,' my father would shout from the yard below if he caught us in full play; wasting winter feed was never tolerated.

Cops and robbers was another popular game. The robbers were always the young ones, hiding to be hunted, never quite strong or fast enough to evade the older children. We would build cross country courses and gallop over them like horses; another occasion when older, longer legs won the day. Block one two three was a regular pastime.[87] Weekends, light nights and holidays, were often spent in let's-pretend land. It was physical play, rope swings and lots of scrambling in trees and bushes, getting nettled, picking dock leaves to alleviate the sting.

This was an environment we roamed and knew intimately: the tapping of a greater-spotted woodpecker as we walked down the lane to the school bus; the hedge where old damson trees hid amongst the tangle of ivy and blackthorn; the holly tree that was sure to bear berries we could bring into the house at Christmas; the hunting gate once used in the days when the land was part of Brough estate; the remnants of a stone byway that ran alongside the land at the bottom of Far field, its destination long replaced by the tarmacked public road that lay two fields south. The hedged boundaries of our land did not hold us in, and the extent of our neighbours' land was like a large moat that separated our community from the villages that lay around us. We were never isolated, but we were separate; we belonged to Tunstall Road, all part of the same gang.

§

---

[87] A game similar to hide-and-seek that involved touching a 'base' before being seen by the person looking for you.

During the summer, my mother played cricket in a local women's league. We sometimes asked to go to a home match on the local sports field but paid little attention to the cricket. Instead, we amused ourselves performing gymnastics, or playing tig as the adult's game got underway. The half-time teas were the real draw and the reason for hanging around rather than staying at home: meat paste sandwiches, sausage rolls, and buttered scones with a blob of strawberry jam on top were a feast. We relished the shop-bought orange juice on offer as anything that was not home-made was considered a treat. The dark luminous orange cordial hummed with the colourants we were told were bad for us.

Invariably the team my mother played for lost. I was seconded onto it when I started secondary school, but despite being good at short distance running I was hopeless at catching and batting. The team captain swiftly moved me into the car on the boundary of the pitch to be a scorer.

At primary school boys and girls had their own entrance to the school which led onto segregated playgrounds. At home on the farms, we all pulled together and gender differences mattered little when we kicked a football about or went on bicycle rides.

§

The butcher called at a neighbour's farm weekly and if we just happened to be hanging around we crowded the back door of his van to be rewarded with half a slice of thinly cut luncheon meat each, quickly dispersing for further games. Little time was spent in each other's houses, the environs of the farms provided all the adventure we needed, and more.

One day we did invite ourselves into a neighbour's small living room, drawn indoors under the spell of coloured wizardry; new technology could not be ignored.

'It's massive!'

'What are all those knobs for?'

'Is there someone in there watching us watching them?'

'Well, I never thought David Bowie had red hair like that.'

Then the arrival of our own television marked a transition in a childhood which, up until this point had been steeped in the exploration of the outdoors and where time inside was mostly spent reading books.

Despite having a new television, mechanisation and consumerism still touched our home little. My mother made our clothes. At primary school I wore a summer dress sewn from a tablecloth she decided she no longer liked. The feeling of self-consciousness when the dress was first worn still lingers, but only my siblings knew its origins, and they kept the secret. Many families managed within similar means. The days of wartime rationing and making do were never far from the minds of my parents' generation.

§

My first kiss was on the Buttertubs Pass, Cliff Gate Road, travelling between Swaledale and Wensleydale when Philip Slater's lips brushed my cheek. We were sat on the back seat of the school bus that was taking our class on a geography field trip. Suddenly it was a rite of passage between childhood and adolescence. The Buttertubs had become an unexpected journey into a new landscape.

Today, returning along this familiar road, this time from Wensleydale into Swaledale, age travelling back into youth, I am aware of the external vastness of land and sky behind me and internalise every rock and cloud ahead.

Formed by limestone erosion, each Buttertub reaches down more than twenty metres. The term is derived from the name given to these natural phenomena by the farmers who rested here on their climb from Swaledale over to the market in Hawes, in Wensleydale. On warm days the butter they carried to sell would be lowered into the deep potholes to cool and prevent it from softening and deteriorating before it reached the market, where the priority was to secure the best price.

Buttertubs, your story seeps away like rain through stone, cools the butter no more. But we must listen to your story because your story is our story too.

Butter - Latin *butyrum*, Greek *bou-tyron*. A chemistry of milk, grass and sun. Myth: milk will not turn to butter if churned by a young woman in love nor by a witch possessing evil spirits.

churn butter churn, come butter come
a little good butter is better than none.[88]

Tub - container: spruce-carved, a butter box. The traditional tools used in hand-made methods of butter-making died away with the advent of mechanisation in the 19th century.

Limestone - sedimentary, carboniferous, organic. An alkaline home to wild thyme, bell heather, juniper and harts-tongue.

Weathering - caves, scars, potholes, paving: rain-stabbed, ice-burnt, heat-shocked, wind-worn, shaft-pushed, rock-cracked, fault-pierced.

The landscape of limestone has two faces: one on the surface, one hidden underneath. Water inhabits both worlds, shaping gills and rock. Under the earth the shy beauty of stalagmites and stalactites link the past with the present; time drips quietly through centuries as they gradually unite to form columns. There is much that is unseen of lives that are shaped by limestone.

§

A major flood can reshape the surface of the land in a matter of hours, weaving new pathways, forging the character of water over the soft pliable ground.

Floods have felled the drystone wall that marks the field to moor. Slack gritstone rives the beck, islands the ash, unleashed from their ribs, headstones and heart stones wrench free.

Five decades ago, the A1 at Catterick flooded badly because the road sat on lower land than the fields that bordered it. There was so much water the carriageways became rivers, enough to row boats and canoes down the fast lanes. This bizarre sight enticed many villagers to the flyover over the road to stand and watch the boat races. Subsequent riverbank reinforcement and new drainage systems were put into place to prevent it happening again.

This 1968 flood was caused by continuous rainfall over a period of days. But in the northern dales in 2019, on a warm July afternoon, the sun was smothered in minutes by the weight of a deluge so fierce that becks and the river Swale were ferocious. This single catastrophic event shaped land and lives in three

---

[88] An example of a traditional butter churning song, with various versions in circulation by the late 19th century.

hours of undiluted force; wrecking homes, sweeping animals downstream, carving up pastures and roads, trampling down walls, spitting its fury without remorse.

Normally somnolent, the landscape was ravaged, nature demonstrating its intransigence. Gills and fell sides became moonscapes, dislodged from themselves by raging water. Boulders were tumbleweed. Gouges of hill sides were scooped up and deposited on the river plain; trees uprooted as though skittles in a game; lives and livelihoods became severed from each other by the usually placid becks that morphed into rapids reeking unforgiving havoc. Water redirected itself through the ground floors of cottages, across businesses, sweeping up cars, depositing them in fields. Centuries old walls crumpled and split their spines in two, offering no resistance to the force of the peat brown torrent. Landlocked villages and towns, along with their communities, found themselves stranded off a coast of fells.

This once in a life-time event is now at the risk of appearing commonplace, inflicting the dale with destruction twice over the last decade. During normal rains, deep gullies rush swiftly into tributary becks and on into the river Swale with ease. But energy-filled clouds affected by a warming climate are monsters. Locals speak of walls of water rushing down the dale. The Swale is one of the fastest rising rivers in England due to the collection of many tributaries falling from the high ground near the source. It has been recorded as rising over three metres in twenty minutes.

Just as the kiss on Cliff Gate Road awakened thoughts I had not contemplated before, so climate change is catapulting humankind into weather events and extinction; a future our ancestors could never have imagined for us.

After the floods of 2019, bulldozers moved in to repair and reorganise some of the affected land and waterways to mitigate the chance of similar devastation again. What has been damaged, the land will eventually heal, if it is given the opportunity without further dramatic climate change.

On the school bus back in 1972 I learned journeys are not about beginnings and endings; it is the small surprises along the way that make life remarkable. Let us hope the children of our children's children will have the freedom to travel through these landscapes and experience their own wonders without the fear that all they have inherited is a broken world.

VOICE
'Pass those names across your tongue as though they were poems'[89]

The landscape of the Yorkshire Dales is charged with language that is written into every farmstead, village green, marketplace, churchyard, descendant.

Swaledale softly tucks her voice into the eastern flanks of the Pennines, speaks the language of water and stone.

If Swaledale is a little country in itself, it is never more so than when considering the vernacular. Each dale has its own variant of dialect words. 'Swua'dle' is the dialect of Swaledale, demonstrated in the traditional method for counting sheep or scoring yows:[90] yahn, tayhn, tether, mether, mimph, hithher, lithher, anver, danver, dic.[91]

Suala is Anglo-Saxon for whirling and rushing. It has the same root as swallow, an apt name for this river, swift flowing even on the calmest of days.

Place names in the dales chart the local history of early Celt, Roman, Anglo Saxon and Viking settlements. The old Celtic word for hill is pen: Penhill in Wensleydale, and Pen-y-ghent in Ribblesdale.

The Romans were not interested in the Yorkshire Dales uplands when they first invaded. However, on discovering the wealth of lead and wool in the area they moved further inland from the main arterial roads. One route they developed on the north-east side of the Pennines veered off Dere Street at Catterick, and ran to Carlisle, Luguvalium.[92] Other roads then branched off along the way, Cam High Road near the fort of Virosidum[93] at Bainbridge,[94] close to Semerwater is an example. Built in the 1st century, this course forms part of a network of crossings from the east to the Roman garrisons in the north-west of England. The road traverses Cam Fell; in the medieval period this was recorded as Kambe road, kame being an Old Scottish word for 'comb', a hill formed from glacial deposits.

---

[89] Andrew Grieg, *At The Loch of the Green Corrie.*
[90] Ewes.
[91] The numbers one to ten used by shepherds for centuries when sheep-scoring. It is thought this method of counting evolved from the Celts.
[92] This road is known as Watling Street.
[93] Virosidum translates as 'settlement beside the River Ure'.
[94] Bainbridge is named after England's shortest river, the river Bain, less than 3 miles long.

Once a route traversed by drovers from Scotland with livestock for southern markets until the railways heralded the demise of this way of life, this remnant from the Romans has left the present day with a pleasant green lane easily accessible from Bainbridge. Now a quiet bridleway, it is the domain of backpackers and walkers until it loses its way on the western side of Ingleton. Centuries of necessity and livelihood have been superseded by leisure and the huge economic benefits this industry now brings to the region.

Semerwater originates from the Old English name for lake, 'mere'. Legend tells of a town underneath the water which was flooded by a poor old man who was declined hospitality by the people. Hungry and begging from door to door he was consistently turned away by all the inhabitants, eventually finding comfort and kindness from a couple who lived in a cottage up the hill from the lake. So disillusioned by his fellow men, he cursed the town asking the water to rise and cover the houses.

Derivations of place names such as Fremington, located over the Arkle beck east of Reeth, come from Anglo Saxon. Fremington has origins in the word for farmstead or village, thought to have been occupied by *Frema's* people, *frema* meaning foreign. *Fremð* was the word for a 'place of strangers'. Evidence of an earlier settlement in the locality was uncovered when two bronze age axe heads were found in the late 1700s.

Healaugh, also mentioned in the Doomsday Book as *Hale*, is derived from the Saxon word *helah*, a stronghold in a forest clearing. This area was once a rich hunting ground where wolves, wild boar and deer attracted the nobility,[95] much as grouse-shooting draws the wealthy to these moors today.

There has been a settlement around the meeting of Swaledale and Arkengarthdale from pre-history. It is possible Reeth's name derives from the earlier Anglo-Saxon word for place by a stream; another theory is that it comes from the word for a place of rough ground. In the Doomsday Book it is entered as Rie. When Reeth received its chartership from William and Mary in 1695, it was not only granted a weekly market but four annual fairs. The Bartle Fair held on or around St Bartholomew's Day,[96] is immortalised in the poem by John Harland, *Reeth Bartle Fair* (1870): 'Thar was dancin' an' feightin' for ever.'[97]

---

[95] A large Norman manor is still evidenced here by a ridge in a field that bears the name 'Hall Garth'.
[96] Patron Saint of Beekeepers, celebrated on August 24th.
[97] Harland, John, 1870, allpoetry.com/Reeth-Bartle-Fair.

On the south side of the dale opposite Reeth lies Harkerside Moor on which you can find the remains of the Iron Age fort, Maiden Castle or Mai Dun.[98] Remarkably, the remains of an avenue of stones leads into the small round fort surrounded by a large ditch into which it is easy to walk. Both ditch and fort are clearly identifiable from the air.

These ancient folds of uplands and dales have been home for hundreds of generations, each in their turn leaving their words woven into the language and habits of their successors. In remote communities such as Swaledale, norms and customs were as intrinsic as breathing. Forebears passed on belief systems that accounted for witches, fairies, malevolent spirits and bad luck; unspoken laws were enforced by self-policing and communal cohesion, the politics of self-preservation. The omniscient eye was never far from the minds of the inhabitants. Stories were passed down from old to young with significance attributed to the smallest incident. At the beginning of the twentieth century Edmund Bogg wrote:

'Born and cradled among the wild and lonely hills, superstition, always the inheritance of the unlearned and isolated mind, fed that as mother's milk does the body.'[99]

I am born from the sinews of these people. My great-grandparents' last name, Alderson, 'older son', is thought to have originated from the earlier pre-Saxon word for 'old army', *ealdhere*. Harker is another last name still prevalent in the dales, from *herkien*, to listen or harken, the occupational name for an early 'police officer' or eavesdropper. The name Swale, or Swales, was given to those who originated from land close to the river.

Some names pass into legend. One such is *Falden Joseph*. After selling his stock at market, this unfortunate drover was murdered for his money whilst crossing the moor heading north beyond Askrigg in Wensleydale. In the days before bank accounts were available to all, setting-off home with your profits in coin was a precarious business. Joseph disappeared and his body was never found; his riderless horse roamed the moor, with no one daring to catch it in case it implicated them in the murder.

§

---

[98] Mai Dun, derived from the Celtic word for ridge.
[99] Bogg, Edmund, *Regal Richmond and the Land of the Swale*, 1909, London: Elliot Stock p. 223.

The river Swale is created by the merging of Birkdale and Great Sleddale Becks. Carved from moorland peat, coarse ling and limestone weathering, the story of the Swale begins as an ancient water-borne track cutting through the dale on which it bestows its name. In its momentum, the river gathers its own folklore and way markers in the form of crossings and waterfalls, wildlife and words written in poetry and song. It is the central character on a vast natural stage conversing with an audience of brown trout, alder, kingfishers, sand martins, willow, steppingstones, coast to coast walkers, ramblers and fly fishermen, and it happily chatters to anyone who will sit on its banks and stay awhile. The river also maps a course beside names that conjure fantasy: Hoggarts Leap, Catrake Force, Oldfield Gutter, Scabba Wath Bridge, The Stell.

Here in Wensleydale an encounter with a signpost, wall and gate, as they converge at a junction. They invite a conversation, a proposition, continuation. Here is a place you might meet earlier incarnations of yourself.

The Vikings who settled in the dales bequeathed their words to the local dialect; many - like *foss*, a waterfall; *garth*, a grassy enclosure; *seat*, upland fields used in summer - still survive. Folded into the landscape are hidden names tattooed onto lichen weathered signposts as though they have been carved by ancient dwellers pointing back into their past; Cotterdale, Raydale, Whitsundale, Bishopdale, Mossdale to name but a few.

Very few people now speak Swua'dle, but some of the vernacular continues to inhabit the local vocabulary and was extensively used in the small community in which I grew up:

barny - an argument, falling out

blether - talk nonsense

capt - amazed

chunterin' - talking under your breath

cuddy wift - left-handed

faffin' - messing around

fettle - mend

gander - look, be nosey

gawp - stare at

golly - bird just hatched, also a term for being naked, bare golly

gripe - fork for spreading/picking up hay, straw and muck

guzzle - eat greedily

lug - carry

maftin' - too hot

mither - bother

recklin - the runt, the weakest animal in a litter

rive rags - as children you were said to be this if you could not sit still

scally - an imp, a rogue, sometimes scallywag

scrow - untidy

shaf - exclamation of disagreement

silin' - raining hard

starved - to be very cold

tew - what you would be in if you were struggling with something

whaffnack - a term used when you did not 'shape up' to a task given

wittler - worrier

§

One late spring afternoon, at the secluded 16th century Ivelet Bridge, an elder of the hamlet stops to chat as we pause to admire the grace of the stone semi-circle arch that forms a full circle when reflected by the river. Shy but majestic, it is a bridge that speaks of harmony:

'Have thee seen th' black dog?'

'Black dog?'

We look at our own black Labs.

'Nay, not these. Theee black dog.'

Our blank expressions encourage the old man to continue:

'Aye. Thee don't want to be seein' him or thee'll be doomed. Folk round here tell that if anyone catches sight of him then death is nivver far behind.'

A coffin stone lies against the wingwall at the northern side of the bridge. It was used to rest coffins on in the days when the dead were brought from the top of the dale at Keld down through the valley and finally through the lychgate of St Andrew's at Grinton and into eternity.[100]

The medieval Swaledale Corpse Way was used by miners, hawkers, farmers and pieceworkers,[101] but this was also the route of the dead. Solemn hymns would be sung as they journeyed down the track, and rituals were played out at bridges and way markers to stop the souls of the deceased following the mourners back up the dale to haunt them.[102] Coffins were made of wicker rather than wood, which was too heavy to carry such a distance, and the cost of a horse and cart too expensive for most bereaved families.

Tread this route today and perchance you might hear the feet of men, women and children fall in beside you, pass the time with you awhile, tell you how little this path has changed in centuries.

Similarly unchanged is Marske valley in lower Swaledale. I walk with the dogs alongside Marske beck, which gently pours itself into the Swale less than a mile downstream. It is easy to merge into this intimate landscape as I look for signs of the changing seasons such as the butterbur, an early returnee with its small pink tassel flowers, happy to be on the damp, cool riverbank. In the sky a tuneful skylark hovers, at first invisible to the eye; patience may be rewarded if

---

[100] St Andrew's is known as the Cathedral of the Dale. After the church of St Mary's at Muker, Upper Swaledale, was built during the reign of Elizabeth I, coffins no longer needed to be brought so far down the dale.

[101] Pieceworkers travelled the farms and were paid for the work they did by the unit, as in potato picking.

[102] This fable comes from Norse mythology.

you catch this small bird dive-bombing towards the ground to settle into the meadow grass.

As I walk the dogs one morning, the crisp March dawn is succumbing to the sun, melting the hoar frost into a soft mellow light, I reflect on who planted the original snowdrops now dying back in the small deciduous copse they carpet; how an aged stone dwelling on the hillside speaks of shelter for the sheep who have wintered out; how the only remnants of Clints Hall[103] is a huddle of cottages, converted stables and the chapel, now a house. All these signify to the passer-by that we live amongst voices of the past.

An old waterwheel beside a millrace is a favourite stop. Even in its dilapidated state, it is a testament to the accomplishments of Victorian craftsmanship; it is a memorial. This is a place to spend some time. A place to reflect. Increasingly, the world exposes us to a kaleidoscope of information where the boundaries of reality are more and more complex and negotiable. But this wheel speaks of simplicity; like an old man leaning on a gate reminiscing and recounting his version of a world that once was before it changed beyond recognition.

Close to the waterwheel we cross a single-track arched stone bridge that spans Marske beck. The dogs run down to the beck to play in the water below. It is one of the oldest crossings in the area and from under the belly of the bridge the single width tells of the days when horses were the engines of farming. Never upgraded for modern machinery and motor vehicles, it has slipped into redundancy other than for the passage of sheep and occasional walkers. The bridge and waterwheel have shared at least one hundred and fifty years of companionship, yet both are so easy to walk past without a second thought.

The 12th century Church of St Edmund King and Martyr sits in the village of Marske, close to the Hall. It takes its name from Edmund, a Saxon King and Saint who was captured and executed by the Danes in AD870, but his is not the only story associated with the Danes on this site.

As the Danish invasion of Lindisfarne, off the Northumberland coast, loomed in about AD793, followers of St Cuthbert rescued his body from Lindisfarne Priory on Holy Island where it had been laid to rest a century before. They set off to carry his remains to safety in Ripon Cathedral, twenty-five miles south of Marske. During their hazardous journey they are said to have rested for a time inside a holy place built on the site on which the church of St Edmund's now stands.[104]

---

[103] Clints Hall was built circa 16th/17th century and demolished in 1843.
[104] St Cuthbert was finally laid to rest in Durham Cathedral.

Externally St Edmund's Church is a solid, weathered building; internally, it reveals pitch-pine box pews, with cream painted interiors and bench seats. Small, hinged doors open the pews up into the aisle. The box for the Marske Hall family sits at the front of the church to the left-hand side of the altar. Raised higher than the pews that grace the aisle and with a larger and taller box frame around it, threadbare blue velvet cushions soften the planed surfaces of the seats. The box was strategic, a symbol of hegemony, positioned so the gentry were closer to the altar - and thus to God - than the common man.

Deference was shown to the squire and his family. The minister may have preached that everyone was equal, but the rich were a little less charitable in their notions of equality. Servants and workers were encouraged to attend the church of their masters in order that an eye could be kept on their whereabouts during the time they were not at their duties. The idiom 'the devil makes work for idle hands' was a concern for the moneyed classes, fearful too much free time would encourage criminality in the lower ranks.

The box pews, circa 1630, the date the church underwent a restoration, transport the visitor back through the centuries. Standing at the entrance, looking down the nave, you can almost hear the wooden clogs of working folk tap the stone flagged floor, the rustle of the 19th century taffeta crinolines as the ladies made their way to the front, the soft hush of cotton and wool worn by ordinary womenfolk as their dresses brushed against the panelled pews. Catch the fading whispers of reverence to a life rooted into an orderly world, everyone fulfilling the role they were born to; the harsh lives of the poor tolerated with fortitude and little hope of changing their circumstances.

§

Other stories hide in the landscape, waiting to be discovered. One such involves a young woman from the Court of Henry VIII: the nineteen-years-old Isabella Beaufort, who fled her role as a Lady in Waiting to Queen Catherine[105] when the King's attentions proved too much for her. Disguising herself as a page, and not wanting to involve her family nor the man she loved because of the danger she may put them in, she found her way north to Marrick Priory, a Benedictine nunnery about three miles east of Reeth.[106] Here the Prioress took

---

[105] Catherine of Aragon.
[106] Marrick Priory was painted by JMW Turner after he came across it on his way to Richmond in 1816.

her in and Isabella sheltered for the years that followed until Henry instigated the dissolution of the monasteries. Around this time, a visiting Prioress from the south of England recognised Isabella and knowing the romantic attachment between her and her former suitor was still very much alive for him, arranged they should be married in secret. Once Isabella was the wife of a nobleman, she was able to leave Marrick under the protection of her husband.

The 12th century Priory stands on flat land close to the River Swale. This gentle scenery, where the river meanders, must have given Isabella a sense of solitude and peace, far removed from court life in London. Bearing north-east uphill from the building are the Nun's Steps[107] which lead through deciduous woodland, a stairway to the small village of Marrick. In summer, boughs arch until the only light is in the shimmering flecks that fall across the path. It is easy to imagine a young Isabella roaming under the freedom of their leafy canopies. Since 1970 the Priory has been used as a youth centre, now an outdoor residential centre for North Yorkshire County Council, having been rescued from life as a farm building.

A few miles downstream, the voices of Downholme village, in Lower Swaledale, stir in the churchyard, telling of families that made this dale their home. The oldest grave is a boxed tomb in dressed stone that has been dated to the medieval period, 13th or 14th century.[108] Most graves pre-date the 20th century when the population in the area was greater. Weathered and worn facades talk of the loss of sisters, aged 26 years and 20 years; John Robinson of Downholm Park[109] who died in 1778; Margaret Carter, who lived, and died a happy death, in 1828; a young wife who was mourned in 1809, aged 23 years; and a daughter that left this life in 1791. The inscriptions are littered with names of families whose descendants still live in the locality.

Downholme church, St Michael and All Angels, dates from the 12th century, but the village of Downholme is mentioned in the Domesday Book by the name of Dune; probably originating from dun, the Anglo-Saxon word for hill. The church sits at the foot of How Hill and was the centre of village life until the Black Death in the 14th century forced the population to flee, burning their houses behind them to prevent further spread. The villagers moved northwards onto the flanks of Seat How,[110] a few hundred yards from the original site, and

---

[107] Used by the Benedictine nuns from Marrick Abbey to provide them with a direct route uphill to the village of Marrick. Today, the steps are included on the coast-to-coast walk.
[108] There are no traces of the identity of who is buried here.
[109] Established as a deer park in 1377.
[110] *How* derives from the Old Norse word *haugr* for hill or barrow. How Hill may be a barrow.

re-built their homes where stone cottages now huddle. Evidence of the rig and furrow of ancient field systems can be seen embossed into the land surrounding the church, especially during the bare winter months or in times of summer drought. History lives in the present.

The layers of landscape; Downholme church is ghosted as the mist clings to the river Swale and spills over the lower ground. Sheep shadow the lower fields whilst the moor-tops burst into focus greeting the light strewn sky.

May. On a ridge above Downholme church the dale becomes an aisle, the sky an altar. This thin place touches the heavens. Here permanency is palpable, human life fleeting. I embrace my own insignificance.

§

In a café in Malton, North Yorkshire, I strike up a conversation with a man on the next table. By coincidence his family came from Ellerton Abbey House:

'My family helped set up the school at Downholme in the early 1800s.'

'They donated £150, about £14,000 nowadays.'

'By the 1840s it was well attended, over thirty children, but that was when workers came to earn a living in the lead mines and the quarry nearby.'

He is a living archive.

By chance, I meet him again when walking the dogs close to the redundant church in Hudswell, also called St. Michael and All Angels.[111]

'I'm still tracing my ancestors.'

---

[111] This village lies approximately 3 miles east of Downholme.

I imagine him wandering in and out of the past, chatting with the people who helped shape this locality. Conversing from their graves, they still have much of interest to pass on. I sense something special; an essence of immortality pervades this second encounter; the shadows we cast after death.

§

A faint inscription above the front door of a cottage in Downholme states: *Good ale to-morrow for nothing. August 10, 1694.*[112]

Today, the Bolton Arms in Downholme is one of three pubs with the same name within a six miles radius. The Lords of Bolton, formerly of Bolton Castle[113] and latterly of Bolton Hall in Wensleydale, once owned all these establishments. When the Ministry of Defence bought land in 1930 to be used as shooting ranges, it acquired Downholme village and the pub; at the time this made it the only pub in England owned by the monarch.

Now in private hands, the Bolton Arms continues to be intrinsic to the cohesion of the community. As in previous decades, locals lean against the bar eager for the exchange of news, just as innkeepers in the past listened to the blacksmith, butcher, wheelwright, shoemaker and agricultural labourer.[114]

Other voices that colour the present vernacular come in the guise of field names. Many were designated because of the practical need to identify land at the onset of enclosure.[115] Naming was often attributed to a previous owner, *Joe's field*, or descriptive, *Long field*. *Well field* at Prospect Farm had a redundant well and a stone water-trough hidden in a small copse in one corner. It is possible that both were strategically sited at the meeting of three fields giving access to the greatest number of farmers with one supply. Or was this the site of a cottage or farmstead that now only leaves traces of itself sketched by water. This borehole in the land, overgrown with grasses, is a place where the imagination can fall through the earth's surface into fathoms of deep time. That it does not provide any answers matters little; it exists as an independent spirit.

---

[112] It was a public house called the King William and closed at the turn of the 19th/20th century. *Swaledale*, Pontefract, Ella, & Hartley, Marie, JM Dent & Sons Ltd: London, 1934, p. 144.

[113] Mary Queen of Scots was held here for a time during her years of incarceration under Elizabeth I.

[114] Census records for Downholme in 1841 list all these occupations against the names of the inhabitants.

[115] Through several Acts of Parliament common land could be bought and enclosed, with the rights of use and access being passed to the new owner. In effect, common land was no longer for communal use.

There is more than one farm or field in the locality called Limekiln after historic workings scattered around the area. They produced burnt lime for the construction of local buildings. In Downholme there is a field called *Neddy's*, named in the early 20th century after a horse that grazed here whilst his owner made one of his regular visits to the pub. Presumably Neddy could find his way home without too much input from his inebriated rider.

Farms were named in much the same manner and those of friends and family need little explanation of their derivation: Oak Tree Farm, Chapel Farm, Hall Farm, Town End Farm and Mount Pleasant Farm. Some names prove more difficult to identify their origins: my mother's cousin lived on a farm called The Nabb, possibly derived from the Viking, *nabbi*, a peak or a knoll; Hundah was the name of my maternal great-grandparents farm, *hund* being the Anglo-Saxon word for a dog used for hunting.

TRACKS
'Nothing still even the dead are on the move '[116]

Hidden by heather and time; fingerposts, a fork in a footpath, a footprint, walking between here and there.

A disused limestone quarry lingered on our land long after the quarrymen had downed tools. It had been worked before memory, now a scoop of scrub adjacent to a track that led to Far Field, a place of dragons and ghouls. If we were feeling particularly brave, we would venture over and play amongst the old stone kilns, the feral elder, ash, alder and spindle.

Once a year, in the spring, a tramp would make his way up our farm lane on foot; alone and unkempt. After a sighting, we were too scared to play in the quarry, knowing he was heading for the shelter it provided. Confirmation he had settled in for a while came when we spotted smoke rising through the trees from a campfire.

'I think he's a child-snatcher, like the one in *Chitty Chitty Bang Bang*.'

'Or a time traveller.'

'Or like the pied piper. Maybe he wants us to follow him.'

'Or the wolf in *Little Red Riding Hood*.'

'What! He's not a wolf. Stupid!'

Our imaginations worked overtime. The vagrant never came up to the farmhouse door or asked anything of us as he passed through. My father and the man shared a silent agreement, the stranger kept himself to himself, and in doing so was not challenged.

The tramp was as timeworn as the lanes and footpaths he wandered. He belonged to the natural world: outside the order of society; not restricted by walls, fences and borders.

He was a red squirrel; as shy as a fallow deer; living in the shadows like the pipistrelle bat. To a child he was a storybook, a sign that summer was on its way, he was 'Walter' because we dared not ask him his name.

---

[116] Mary-Jane Holmes, *B6276*.

'Where do you think he comes from?'

'Over yon hill I'd say.'

'Noooo, where does he really live?'

'Nowhere, I guess. He may have been a soldier in the war.'

'Does that make him a gypsy?'

Excited by danger, we were intoxicated with the idea he was someone who was living outside of all we were told was normal.

'No, he's a poor divel that's had a rough ride through life.'

'Shell-shock maybe. He's an old man and he does us no harm.'

'Don't go botherin' him. Leave him to get on with himself.'

Looking back, he may have been a military veteran; in those days so many soldiers from both World Wars led displaced lives due to the lack of understanding of mental health conditions such as post-traumatic stress disorder.

Every year he shadowed the stack yard wall as the bare wood of blackthorn danced with blossom. He lumbered on potholed leather, the slide of life in the slope of his shoulders as the soft south-westerlies blew him through. Some years father would announce at teatime:

'Old Walter passed through today.'

He was a pebble in a stream, tumbled and bruised, raking in and out of the reeds.

One evening, a stranger appeared, unsettling the security of our hill at the end of a long, warm June day. My father was out at a NFU[117] meeting; my mother was alone downstairs whilst we slept in our beds. Suddenly, at the kitchen window, a man jumped into view glaring in at her and brandishing my father's old scythe with its long, curled blade, used to cut nettles and thistles in the pastures. The man was scruffy and ill-shaven; his demeanour agitated and threatening. Quickly locking the house door, my mother rushed to phone for assistance from Joseph next door. By the time help arrived, the man had disappeared. Like the tramp who passed through regularly, this younger man might have been a veteran too; the second world war had ended twenty-five years earlier.

The idea of a bogeyman struck fear into us and was a term my grandmother frequently used when she was looking after us.

---

[117] National Farmers Union.

'Do as I tell you or the bogeyman will steal you away, and then what will I tell your mother?'

Derived from hobgoblins, boggarts or bogles, these mysterious spirits ranged from the mischievous to malevolent intentions.

'You don't want to be upsettin' them. When they are angry, dogs get ill, the cream turns sour, they can even make things disappear without warnin'. Including children.'

Her voice lowered as she conveyed the last part of this warning. It was enough to assure our compliance and best behaviour.

In previous centuries, pagan beliefs required that communities set aside a piece of land for these little sprites to inhabit; then, with luck, they would refrain from bothering anybody. Place names derived from words like nick and puck[118] reflect this myth. Scarth Nick is a steep incline and wooded area on the outskirts of Redmire in Wensleydale, a name that may have roots back in these superstitions. Malice End, in the locality of Tan Hill, is another dark name upon which to speculate.

§

Travelling women and girls called now and then with their wicker baskets full of primitively carved wooden pegs. My mother was resilient to their sales pitch and having her fortune told; my father less so and would buy something however small. These visitors were intriguing. Often, they appeared in late May or early June as they passed through with their menfolk on their way to Appleby Horse Fair in Cumbria. The jaunty domed caravans bobbed along the hedgerows to the tune of dogs barking at each farm gate they passed: an incessant early warning system, alert and ready to sound the alarm of strangers nearby. By evening, the coloured horses that pulled the caravans would be tethered on verges up and down local lanes. Next day they would harness up and move on, meandering the dales, wind in their faces as they continued their journey westwards over Bowes Moor.

Sighting of this nomadic community created a nervous inquisitiveness in us. This was purely based on difference. Our existence was static; even if events happened out of our parents' control there were ways and means of dealing with them that restored equilibrium swiftly.

---

[118] Shakespeare's 'Puck' - Robin Goodfellow in *A Midsummer Night's Dream* is an example.

'It's common sense.'

This was my mother's mantra that explained everything she agreed with and was used as a reprimand when she did not. But travellers were about movement, roaming and adventure. To our young way of thinking it lacked sense to take every possession you owned with you wherever you went.

'How can anyone fit their house into such a small caravan?'

'I have no idea.'

This answer was not enough to sate our curiosity.

'It must be like a deep cave. Or like in Doctor Who. A Tardis.'

If this was the case, then gypsies were very frightening. Doctor Who and the Daleks where the scariest thing on television.

'It must be bigger than it looks once you're inside.'

'Where do they live in winter?'

'Why don't they stop somewhere and just stay there?'

'Can we get a caravan?'

Sometimes we were not given answers to our questions. It was unsettling when neither parent could provide a logical explanation.

Irish road workers called if they had any materials left over from road resurfacing at the end of their day. This happened frequently when the A1 was being upgraded. These lilting, dark-haired men went from farm to farm trying to sell their sticky pungent tarmac and aggregate stones, chatting everyone into knots, bartering for cash in hand. They were pedlars, selling their wares, living by their wits, just as so many have done in the past.

Once or twice we did buy from the Irish to fill the pot-holed farm lane which had to be kept free of standing water as it was our path to and from the school bus each day. The bus stopped at the end of our lane. Here several families congregated; mothers accompanying their infants until they were six or seven years old, seeing them onto the Leyland bus owned by Percival's who had a depot on Catterick Camp four miles away.[119]

Percival's was a dales company founded in 1937, closing in 1971, but it was not the first bus service in Swaledale. In 1905 a post-bus route began to run a return service between Richmond and Keld, which continues in a similar guise today.

---

[119] Originally known as Richmond Camp, Catterick Camp was founded in 1914 in response to the outbreak of the First World War. Now known as Catterick Garrison, it is the largest British Army base in the UK and Europe.

Mrs Whyte, the motherly headmaster's secretary, lived on our route to school. She sat on the front seat of the bus making sure all the waifs picked up from outposts along the roadside were safely deposited at school and dropped off at home later in the day. This was all part of an extended service.

Another servant of the community was the mole catcher who lived quietly on the edge of our village.[120] He followed the secretive tracks of the mole, instincts attuned to the world of the soil that lay just below the surface. The mole, a tiny velveteen creature, tunnels as far as twenty metres per day, throwing up molehills and contaminating grassland and silage crops with bacteria that can harm cattle and sheep. Sometimes a row of dead moles can be seen strung along a wire fence on a farm lane or in a field. Their black lifeless bodies hang like trophies in a cabinet, a testament to the success of the catcher and as proof, for payment, of how many have been caught at any one time.

My mother tells of trapping moles as a child and sending their pelts off in the post to receive three old pence per skin in return. Because of its durability and weatherproof qualities, moleskin cloth has been used since Roman times to make clothes such as trousers, jackets, and other country-wear. This was before the arrival of cheaper mass-produced synthetic fabrics.

Our mole catcher was an elderly man, still practicing a skill that had been passed down to him by his father and grandfather. Widely recognised and respected in the community for his expertise, he quietly executed his job alone. A little like the mole itself, he worked under the cover of dusk setting his metal traps. The blood of his forebears ran through him telling him which run a mole was working, which runs were redundant. But moles are canny and no respecters of walls and boundaries and so can remain uncaught as they work their way under the land, clever enough to sense when a human may be on their trail.

§

Swaledale is populated with miles of frayed lanes and bridleways linking steady market towns, villages gathered around their greens, hamlets hanging onto hillsides, hardy farmsteads braided into walls and moors.

The Ice Age carved swathes of valleys running east-west, meaning that most settlements from Keld to Reeth recline on the north side of the dale to take

---

[120] In some rural areas moles are called mowdies.

advantage of the warmth of the sun on the days it shines. Ancient drover's lanes still lace the land, although countless are only partially visible as their walls tumble and merge into pastureland; many just run out of track and disappear from memory. The most recently built routes follow the bottom of the dales. Highways of the past dawdled higher up the fell-sides unaware that the appetite for cars and motorbikes would eventually make their inclines too challenging.

Over centuries, villages and farmsteads also disappeared, and so byways changed their courses, leaving behind the stones of abandoned homes. My sister and I set out from Surrender Bridge[121] on a pilgrimage to Low Cringley one blustery December afternoon to pay a visit to our great-great-great grandmother.

Uphill, until the broken walls that were once your home cloy us into peat bound clots of asphodel, queen of the underworld, happy to swallow our feet, root us into the stories you carry.

We come to find you in this skin of ruin; in lives never known. Except for blood, we are strangers, divided by the long dead, the half living, the unborn.

We have followed the map tracing us back to your hearth, where our women and men birthed and died; an invisible thread binding us to the names we meet.

Here, on this furrow of earth, we touch the old flue where your fire once burned, feel the pulse of your limestone; look through your frameless windows into the bones of winter, the dogwood and willow, scarred and tired, done with an old year.

Standing on your threshold, we talk to you of the way the moor parts into a gill on the south side of the dale; how the starless nights are so dark, entombed in an eternity of emptiness.

You laugh at us when we tell you, this is what we most fear.

§

Drive the high road westwards out of Richmond and drop down into the quiet village of Marske resting in a hollow. Out of Marske take the road towards Marrick. Just past the second signpost turning left for Marrick a sudden release of upland spreads across the eye. From here Swaledale stumbles over and over itself into the distance, resounds with sounds of ancient settlements: Angram, Oxnop, Crackpot, Strands. Room after room of secret passages

---

[121] On Reeth High Moor between Langthwaite in Arkengarthdale and Low Row in Swaledale.

leading on to Great Pinseat, West Stonesdale, Garsdale, and south towards Wensleydale, Nidderdale, Upper Wharfedale and beyond. Similarly, the road over Grinton Moor from Leyburn invites the wanderer to stop at its highest point and embrace the tip of the brow before it descends; feel the communion of Swaledale and Arkengarthdale with Calva hill rising from the centre lending its presence to both dales.[122]

Looking in a westerly direction up Swaledale with the village of Gunnerside south-east of centre in the photograph. Walls and barns patchwork the landscape on the lower flanks of the dale. In the far distance is the wide and flat-topped Great Shunner Fell, thought to mean 'Big Lookout Hill'. At 716m it is the 3rd highest point in the Yorkshire Dales and marks the watershed between Swaledale and Wensleydale.

In late spring and early summer, the circular Muker to Keld walk takes pleasure in the wildflower meadows before crossing to the north bank of the river, following the valley known locally as the Swale Gorge to the old mining village of Keld. This hamlet was once teeming with miners, now coast to coast walkers and day trippers can chance upon the barn and old school which house a treasure of recollections, history and artefacts that record when it was a flourishing community.

---

[122] Calva, or Calver hill is also known as Reeth Low Moor and is littered with the spoils of mining.

Grey faces stare down from boards of old photographs directly into our own; straight mouthed and leaden, reluctant to let us go.

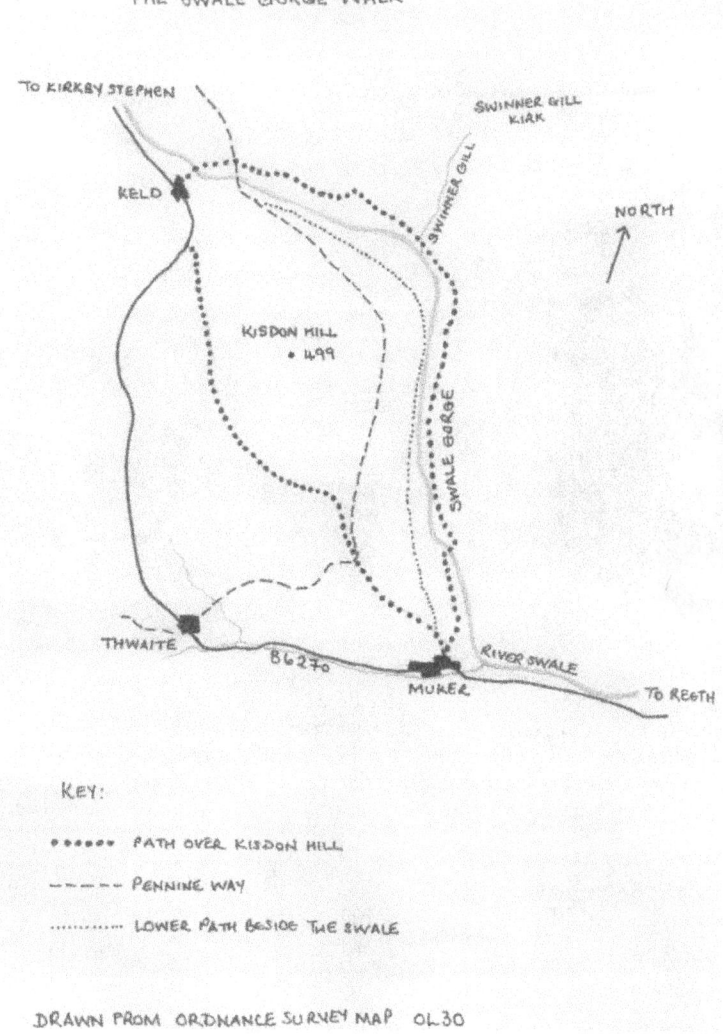

We begin our gorge walk at Muker, strolling through the meadows to the river with the dogs. As sunshine soothes the rough edges of early April, we inhale the air cleansed by the frost and northerlies of winter. Catkin buds stretch on birch-spread arms. Along our way pheasants voice their disapproval at our intrusion. An inquisitive bumble bee interrupts our thoughts now and then. The dogs know this path, mooch the familiar mulch of peat under damp wooded banks, squelching knee high, stirring the musk of the earth. The air smells of fertility: rich, alluvial and vital.

A steady incline pulls us out of the valley, and nudge by nudge the sight of Keld unfurls in the distance. The hamlet feels unchanged, static, the hustle of pubs and miners long gone. All that remains is for this squat of cottages to nestle in for centuries of rest, with nothing better to do than encourage visitors to stand and absorb the vistas that surround it. Keld is oblivious of what might be over the hill or around the next corner. It speaks of waterfalls and limestone scars.

Explore above the slumbering dwellings and watch the moor break free, running wildly onto the higher fells where the sky and land meet head-on. We stop to absorb the energies and rhythm of the land; the dogs look at us before they turn their heads as if a glimpse of this unleashed upland has made their walk worthwhile too.

The return from Keld to Muker can be made on one of three footpaths. The lower path is easy to find, keeping mostly to the pastures that accompany the Swale on the south side of the river. The middle path, along North Gang Scar, follows the renowned Pennine Way. But, for an elevated, panoramic view, take the footpath off the road just east of Keld over the top of Kisdon Hill. On a cloudless day this route will never disappoint. At the summit, stop, embrace the air and soar. The reward; a majestic view floating eastwards.

Kisdon Hill is independent, standing free of its Pennine parents, severed by retreating glaciers; an island in the middle of the Swale on the east and Skeb Skeugh,[123] Thwaite and Straw becks to the west.

In early summer the pastures below Kisdon are carpets of protected flora, safe from the blade of the grass-cutter until they have set their seed. Flecks of yellow, white, cream, pink, orange and purple usurp gentle grasses, making each field an asterism, a galaxy, a universe; each diminutive petal caught in a vastness.

Nature's tapestry is timeless: meadowsweet, buttercup, eyebright, betony, lady's mantle, daisy, melancholy thistle, meadow crane's-bill. But it is human influence that has brought these pastures so near to the brink of destruction. Mechanisation has diminished these meadows by destroying the natural course

---

[123] Skeb Skeugh is a beck. The name is thought to be derived from Norse, but the meaning is unknown. It is just over 2 miles long.

they need to re-establish themselves in preparation for the following spring. Now, the delay in haymaking allows for seeding before the cutting begins and means conservationists and farmers are actively sewing these fields into the future.

These meadows have SSSI, Site of Special Scientific Interest, and SAC, Northern Pennine Dales Meadows Special Area of Conservation protection.

BONES
'we hold all our days in our bones'[124]

Swaledale sheep are hardy little curly-horned animals with a distinctive black head and white rimmed eyes and muzzle. Their faces are amiable and inquisitive, with bodies of thick wool the colour of limestone. Their bones are the minerals of the moorland on which they graze. Sometimes, beside a wall, you might stumble across a dead rabbit, stoat, or an old Swaledale sheep that has not survived into another spring, now giving themselves back to the land.

There are days when my father talks of bones, ploughing up a ewe's skull, sheep on his hands, the sigh of a lamb on his tongue, each gimmer, tup, breathing the same soil, bones from the same fell.

An elderly Swaledale tup stands with the Methodist chapel in Keld behind him. The gravestones are a reminder of the interdependence between sheep, faith and the generations of folk who hail from this westerly edge of the dale.

---

[124] Nick Pemberton, *the transparency of shadows*.

The interdependence of sheep and farmers in these uplands cannot be exaggerated. Shepherd and flock weave together, heft to each other. Maps of the dales are scattered with old stone sheepfolds, as if tattooed onto the skin of the earth. Wool, like a scratch of clouds in a grey sky, snags on splintered gateposts. Wintering on the fellsides, the ewes' rumps are coloured with the tup's raddle, red-ochre, deep green or blue,[125] brightening the lengthening daylight, their bellies budding for spring.

Swaledales are not a pure breed. Like man, over time they have travelled from other regions to make the moorland their home. Once they were believed to be descended from Argali, a tough mountain sheep of Central Asia, but it is more likely that they are derived from the Blackface and Rough Fell sheep of Scotland and northern England.

§

Frank's farm was a short drive away from ours. Loaded up with a trailer full of Bluefaced Leicesters, sheep dipping was worth a trip out with my father. Frank was a bachelor and a tenant of Home Farm, which sat within view of the parkland that surrounded a small, square Georgian country house, Wardby Hall. Frank's farmhouse was situated behind the main house and had long ago been painted a mellow saffron; now the colour flaked from the walls, peeling back to expose the stone-grey of old age. It sat in a rebellious garden that just about managed to contain the flowers, fruit trees and weeds within its walls. The farm buildings were equally unruly, a group of stables and fold-yards, once grand, now unkempt and in need of a hammer and nails. Wooden hen huts hovered around the fringes of the farmstead whilst Golden Comet hens scratted for spilt oats, at times venturing into the front field over which an open track rambled, leading the visitor from the public road.

The sheep dip was close to the farmstead end of this track, enclosed by a rubble of wall and wooden hurdle-fences which were moved backwards and forwards to let sheep through the dip's one-way system: in, down through the pit of stinking, murky creosote soup, up and out the other side. The construction was so narrow that once inside the sheep had no alternative but to proceed through, and, with a push from Frank's long metal rod fashioned for the purpose, suffered the consequences of being immersed before scrambling out. My father

---

[125] A ram wears a raddle harness strapped to his body. It holds a block of coloured wax or oil-based marker on his underbelly. This rubs onto the backside of each ewe so the shepherd can see when she has been covered.

operated the gate to direct the animals through one by one. We were given the job of letting each of the dip-shocked animals out, watching as they bolted across the field as if blasted from the barrel of a gun.

It was a procedure followed so many times that the men worked automatically as they chatted, laughing in companionship, continuously assessing the good, bad and ugly of the sheep world. Occasionally they were interrupted when an unwieldy ewe decided to play up and object to the procedure a little more forcefully than her sisters. From an early age my siblings and I were well versed in expletives from occasions such as this.

The purpose of dipping is two-fold: to control scab mites, ticks and other disease-bearing parasites that live on the skin of the sheep, but also to stain the wool the desired shade, a sandy hue, so the animals looked their best at the late summer agricultural shows and autumn sheep sales.

Shearing was an annual summer event on the sheep calendar. Fuelled with testosterone, two locals in their early twenties travelled from farm to farm working through flocks. The ewes were gathered into a makeshift pen in the yard and one by one my father fed them through a gate system to the shearers. The men were efficient, their mechanical shears working deftly, denuding each animal of its fleece. A neighbour - or my brother when he was older - would let each ewe out through a gate after the shearers were finished with them, gathering the fleeces up and throwing them out of the way onto dry concrete. Later, each fleece, known as greasy-wool when it is bought straight from the farm, would be rolled and stored in the pig-hole until they were collected by the wool-merchant who bought from most farms around us.[126] Loud chat and much good humour accompanied the stench of sheep muck and body odour as the men toiled. It was a job for the height of summer, before harvest started, meaning arduous work for all concerned on a muggy day, resulting in grime-smeared faces.

It was a scene from which we stood back, feeling detached from the internal codes of alpha conversations. My father enjoyed such occasions. His Northumbrian accent became accentuated amongst the heightened camaraderie. His belly laugh rose from his boots and shook his body; a bonding we did not understand but felt sharply in our own bellies too.

---

[126] Wool prices in the 1960s and 70s was guaranteed to provide 10%-15% of the income from sheep. In recent decades prices have dropped below 5% as demand from large markets like China has fallen away, making the cost of shearing more than the price farmers receive for the wool. A revival is now being led by the green industry, for example where wool is used as house insulation and in the mechanical gears for wind turbines.

The pull towards visiting Frank's farm was not sheep alone. Frank was a horse man. This marked him out amongst my father's peers. Cattle and sheep farmers were not known for their love of these grass-guzzling animals, at least not in our community of small-holdings where grass was a precious commodity.

In a leather-bound album, between sheets of tracing paper, a black and white photo of a young woman on a horse spoke to me; both horse and rider looked smart and alert. It was a picture of my mother to which I returned often as my sister and I yearned for a pony of our own.

We pestered our parents; the love of horses, and the desire to ride, was in our blood and encouraged by Frank, despite my father's protestations. In the absence of a pony, we acquired a redundant saddle pad,[127] and threw it across a wide stone wall in the farmyard, attaching a length of billy band in a loop around the fence that met the wall. This string was our reins and we spent many hours riding the wall: competing in pony club competitions, point-to-pointing over miles of open ground, jumping the most challenging hedgerows. Later, when we finally got our own way and my father succumbed and allowed us to have a real pony, we discovered that we had been providing much amusement to Tommy and his son.

'Buy th' lasses a pony Robbie.'

He lobbied on our behalf.

'We've got a bet on who'll get that stubborn old wall to gallop out the yard first. But it ain't shiftin' fast.'

He laughed at his own joke.

We started with an aged, bomb-proof grey called Daisy, which Frank lent to us to see if we retained the initial keenness. Daisy was less than nimble, kind natured, but soon became a plodder as we galloped ahead of her with enthusiasm. My father could not now reign us in, and a series of ponies became part of growing up as my sister and I progressed steadily as riders, setting up our own show-jumping and cross-country courses, hacking out in the lanes around the farm.

A family friend asked me to back a wick[128] pony that had got the better of his daughter. The spritely dapple had the wind in his eye and instantly tried to intimidate me. Having none of his silliness, he soon realised I was more than a

---

[127] A saddle pad is used in the process of breaking in a pony or horse. It is soft and light, ours was made of a thick felt, and allows the young animal to become used to having a saddle strapped onto its back before a heavier leather saddle is introduced.
[128] Colloquial for nimble, quick.

match. The understanding that passed between us was an adrenalin kick for me, the like of which I had rarely felt in my brief years.

On a visit to Home Farm soon afterwards, Frank called me aside:

'I've got a nice young pony for you.'

I followed him through to an open yard where a piebald's[129] stare caught mine with a directness that told me to be wary. Frank placed a saddle pad on her back, tying the girth.

'Right up you get then and walk her 'round.'

I offered a leg and was hoisted aloft and onto the pony's back, grasping the bridle reins with care so I did not make a sudden movement and scare her. After two or three times around the small arena Frank came clean.

'Well, you're the first person to back her properly.'

The fold yard was enclosed, so neither of us could go far or fast, but I felt a thrill of delight in communing with this animal in this small space.

'What does she feel like?'

'Like standing in the front row of a Roxy Music concert waiting for Brian Ferry to come out.'

'Aye. She's a gud 'un and we'll make a rider of you yet.'

This was a compliment indeed from a plain-speaking man.

Being a bit of a dealer, Frank bought ponies and broke them in before selling them on. Now, every school holiday I cycled the eight miles round-trip to watch and learn the craft of breaking horses. It was a pleasure I shared with another girl, Liz, one of a few who kept their own horses in a do-it-yourself livery at Home Farm.

There was a lake in the grounds of Wardby Hall, and on hot days Liz and I would take two of the more experienced ponies and ride into the water to swim, with only a rope halter to control each animal. As we waded in, the motion of the horse's suppleness in graceful and confident movements could be felt through their rippling back muscles and into our own bodies. It was a joyous and simple connection between horse and human. But for me it was much more than this; it encapsulated the desire to be released from the restraints that increasingly seemed, as a developing teenager, to frustrate my days. I wanted to let go of everything that constrained me and gallop bareback.

---

[129] The term for horses with black and white markings.

Horses exude muscle and strength, yet the greatest pleasure is to rest your face in their mane, feel the silk of their coat against your cheek, inhale their musk; their scent remains on your hands and clothes, on your breath, long after you have left them.

The local hunt held a point-to-point every spring at Wardby Castle. The day was, and remains, a social event on the calendar for many enthusiasts. Some years our parents would take us along. The delight of standing around the ring pre-race, watching the athletic thoroughbreds pace the circle, snorting with anticipation of the race to come, released an urgency into our youthful bodies too.

But this was another world from which I felt detached. The uniformity of tweed-skirted women and trench-coated men was a club that seemed exclusive; their talk was indecipherable, despite it being of horses and sport. Betting stands were an unfathomable language too. I watched with fascination as the odds were chalked up, rubbed out, chalked up again and cash was exchanged in handfuls. Tic tac[130] was mesmerising. Phrases such as 'on the nose' when a horse was backed to win, or the betting configurations of the Round-Robin or Yankee were bewildering. Everyone in our group studied the race-card which gave the current racing form of all the horses running, before picking one by the name we liked or the colour of the horse that appealed to us regardless of the odds. This way we never went home with a great win, only degrees of loss measured against others in our party.

The most exciting part of the day was to run to the top of the high ground in the centre of the course as soon as the horses made their way to the start. The course commentator twisted the glorious sounding names around his tongue, Purple Peter, Laughing King, End of the Island, a stream of fantastical imagery. 'And they're orfff.'

From then on, all words were impossible to comprehend as the horses raced in and out of the megaphone. We followed the colours of the jockey's silks, willing our favourites on as they approached the winning post as if our enthusiasm could help bring in the winner too.

Later, at home, I would tack up my pony, Pepsi, and take her to the longest field on the farm to mimic the races I had watched earlier. She and I understood each other perfectly when we were out together alone. In the furthest corner on the farm we would turn, and giving her only the slightest squeeze to encourage,

---

[130] Hand signals used by bookmakers to convey the odds for each horse across to fellow bookmakers.

she would take off and fly, the sound of her hooves in tune with my heartbeat. Our sinews were one; the exhilaration from speed was a joy. Pepsi taught me that the best relationships we make in life are often based on moments of sharing.

The dance of an Arab horse is seductive, dramatised by the graceful lift of their feet, their exaggerated manner of stepping out, tail held in elegance, aloft from their hind quarters like a glorious tassel. Known for an abundance of spirit and intelligence, they are regularly crossed with other breeds, producing offspring that often retain these Arab characteristics.

Such a pony called Wharton spent a little time with us on the farm, until the day he took fright at a fertiliser bag caught in the breeze. Breaking free from his lead rein he stampeded down our garden path in fright. Fortunately, a visiting friend was quick-witted enough to snatch my toddler brother from under his legs in a split second that might have proved catastrophic. This incident confirmed my father's doubts about having ponies on the farm; the ruminations on their place amongst us weighed heavy around our kitchen table.

LOSS
'nothing lasts, everything belongs'[131]

Riding was a pastime not without danger and sadly did provide my first experience of tragic death. A young schoolfriend rode another friend's pony out one day when it spooked at a passing car, she slipped from the saddle catching her foot in the stirrup as she fell. As she fought to release herself, the bolting pony dragged the wisp of a girl with appalling ease, and in the panic, she fatally hit her head on a stone post on the west side of the flyover above the A1. The pony was caught unharmed, but the village felt the despair of the family on the loss of such a young life. The accident rippled across the pool of every home in the district.

Death was normalised by our experiences with the animals; it was part of the cycle that encompassed us. The death of a cow or sheep left no time to dwell on its consequences; farmers did not invest in reflection, stoical attitudes and few displays of regret or sorrow ever slipped from their lips.

'It's happened, move on.'

But Nicola's death was shocking beyond any notion of cyclical continuation and renewal. It was sudden and callous; a freak accident that left a village in mourning. Happening in my early teens, this heart-breaking death stayed with me, anchored itself into every day. I started to question the cocoon in which we lived, one that had seemed so safe, not least because it was lodged solidly in certainties. I felt dislocated. Mortality began to interrupt the security of home and what remained of my childhood. The notion of transience, the fragility of everything I had thought was a constant became a morbid preoccupation.

'You're just being silly.'

My mother applied common sense when I tried to explain how I felt.

'You have to pull yourself together. Everyone dies sometime. You, me, everyone.'

I retreated into my own thoughts and tried to cope with the anxiety.

Thursday July 1st 1976 was warm and promising much for the rest of the day. The end of term exams were over, school was stretching and yawning, unfurling its limbs in anticipation of the long summer break. On this morning I was late setting out for the school bus. As I scurried down the farm lane,

---

[131] Chris Powici, *Wester Glen Almond*.

neighbouring youngsters, including my own siblings, had already boarded the bus as it waited for me. Flanked by a hedgerow overgrown with wild carrot and dog rose that spilled over onto a verge thick with hedge parsley and hogweed, a car tucked in to avoid the stationary vehicle as I approached the rise to the road. In the tangle of tall stems, the driver failed to see me before it was too late.

'Something inside made me watch you all the way down the lane.'

My mother recounted to me later in the hospital.

'When the car hit you I saw you flung up into the air. It was like a bad dream. For a few seconds I didn't believe what I had seen. Then...'

'Then I knew that you had hit the bonnet of the car. I saw you lying in the road... but too far away to see how hurt were.'

'I ran. At first it was as though I couldn't run fast; it was all in slow motion like I had weights tied to my ankles. But I kept running and calling your father. I could see the car, thankfully it had stopped, a green mini, a woman was kneeling beside you. A nurse. Her uniform became clear as I got closer. She'd been coming off nightshift, but oh what a state she was in, sobbing and sobbing.'

'Someone, I forget who, had already run to Tommy's to call an ambulance.'

'I remember the car windscreen, shattered and you lying in all the glass. And the blood...'

My final bounce from the car bonnet left my soft young body a little more dented than the car.

'There was so much blood...so frightening.'

it began with speedwell   forget-me-not   bindweed   mown grass   innocent
verges   maybe   a buzzard mewing blue   a rook   or two
dust stirred potholes   the taste of drought
September remained on the far side of harvest   beyond promises of
the youth club disco   Matthew Harvey's mouth on mine
it ended at the school bus   a waiting driver   drumming dalliance
clock blown dandelions   watching the seconds   the   slow   slowing
slow road   that rises   above my head   then   the slowly fall
into spitting brakes   metal-glassed-flesh   tar-ripped-bone
before   nothing   nothing   but   a distant autumn
caught   in the blur of a siren

When the headmistress visited me in hospital a few days later, she told how every child that witnessed the accident from the bus had needed to go straight into sick bay when they arrived at school.

Returning in the autumn term, I was the centre of attention for a day or two, pulling back bandages to show the scarring from injuries and the subsequent operations on my left forearm. I recounted to many audiences the list of bones that had been broken, the teeth I had lost, the number of stitches used to sew me up, how I had needed a metal plate in my arm.

The council widened the lane end shortly afterwards and the hedge was replaced by posts and rails to ensure good visibility in future. On the day, one of my shoes was missing and remained so until the winter morning Tommy opened a bale of hay whilst feeding stock and it fell out like a coin from a Christmas pudding. The grass in the field on the left-hand side of the road had been cut for hay on the day before the accident. The shoe had been gathered up by the baler and hidden away for months before the bale was cut open, much like the flashbacks that haunted me long after the incident.

What remained inside me from that day went unnoticed by my parents and teachers. The internal upheavals, triggered by my friend's death and given greater fervour by the accident, provoked a response of over-caution and introversion; a worrier continually struggling with panic attacks. The fear of stepping outside our back door and something random happening was a constant. No longer invincible, I had walked out of the house one morning and come too close to accidental death. Innocence dissipated in the trauma of those two incidents. It was the end of childhood as I had known it.

Stress became my companion and narrowed my world. On medical advice I had to give up riding, outdoor play and sports for a year due to the fear of falling and causing greater damage to my initial injuries. By the time all my activities could resume, fearfulness was ingrained and there was little appetite for adventure.

Cattle and sheep trample the same route backwards and forwards through their pastures, and in time these form definite paths, worn with purposeful direction, to the field gate, to water, to food troughs. My paths became much like these. I did not stray from surety and safety. I was like a mole underneath the surface of the earth, carrying out the function of living by digging myself tunnels, throwing up angry soil as evidence I was passing through. Home was a forum for venting a quiet rebellion. In burying down into books, I was safe; I could live adventures between the pages, write about them, read about them, yet have no need to confront danger, or other people.

'Are you coming to the youth club?'
'Not this Friday.'
'Why? You never come. You promised. You always back out at the last minute.'
'You're never going to let your hair down if you don't start to join in with us.'
Tense and tight, I shrugged my shoulders in response. Then, after my 'O' levels, something, somehow, sowed a seed, instigated a fight back, maybe the change of school or a maturing mind, and I began to try harder to fit back into the teenage life of which my peers were making the most. A boyfriend, sleepovers with girlfriends, learning to drive; the future began to build itself. However, the impact of the accident remained an adversary for years into adulthood; inner conflicts became adept at hiding themselves behind an outward veneer of mock confidence.

Mental health was a subject that remained largely unspoken about in the culture of the 1970s. My parents discussed it now and then in the context of one neighbour, their hushed tones suggested finality: an irretrievable state of mind.

'Well, you know he's had a nervous breakdown.'
'Oh, he's never going to be the same again.'

Our farming community's pragmatic outlook on life did not indulge those who suffered from what was then termed as 'nerves'. Empathy was never excessive; any pity was reserved for the families of those suffering.

Farming is often determined by factors out of an individual's control, such as weather, disease and prices for stock, with implications that are huge in relation to profit margins and subsequent financial stress. Farming is, and was then, often lonely and isolating, problems were buried rather than confronted. With small family-run farms, long working hours and minimal social interaction, there was an increased probability that depression could culminate in serious illness. Other factors, like exposure to pesticides before stricter laws and bans on certain substances were brought in, are thought to have had a direct impact on health. Thankfully today there is greater awareness, and networks are in place for those who need to talk or require advice and support before rural issues become a crisis; but as an industry, farming remains a profession in the top ten of the suicide league table.

§

Again and again, farming displays an outer face and hides an inner reality. The turn of the year into spring provides renewal and hope, but behind the glorious display deeper concerns for the welfare of animals, plants, birds and insects can be measured by their decline. The rare breeds list is littered with farm animals that were once commonplace.

The long-wooled Teeswater, which hails from Teesdale in County Durham and looks a little like the Afghan Hound of the sheep world, was popular with my father's contemporaries as a crossing sire with Swaledales to produce the Masham. These hardy animals, with fleeces that were once sought for spinning, now sit on the at-risk register. Wool is imported from countries such as Australia, synthetic fibres are cheap, and pre-made clothes from Asia cheaper still.

The dusty roan coats of the Northern Dairy Shorthorn were a common sight in our neighbour's fields in the 1960s and 70s. Kept for their ability to manage themselves outdoors in all seasons with the bonus of being good milkers and easy calvers, as the dairy farms disappeared so they too have slipped onto the critical list with less than one hundred and fifty purebred cows surviving at present.

The Dales pony is a native northern breed whose working history was integral to lead mining in the Yorkshire Dales until the industry's demise. Being strong and amenable in character, Dales ponies carried the lead in packs of up to one hundred and ten kilograms from the mining sites in Upper Swaledale down into Richmond, covering a great deal of rough ground with remarkable speed and sure-footedness. Unfortunately today their dark stocky frames are a rare sight grazing the fields in and around their traditional upland habitat. They are a noble animal with wonderful full manes that fall over the right-hand side of their necks, and bright jet eyes, but their appealing demeanour is not enough to save them from the risk of disappearing altogether.

My mother's parents bred and showed Clydesdale horses on their farm near Northallerton. A Scottish breed, they are draught horses: strong, heavy and purposeful; gentle giants with soulful eyes. They were used on the land for ploughing, pulling carts and general heavy work before the invention of the diesel engine.

Horse brasses hung on our farmhouse walls in the same way as they once adorned the Clydesdales' leather harnesses. These small plaques depicting the sun, moon and stars were thought to ward off evil spirits, ensuring the fertility of the land the horses ploughed. Sadly, the power of the spirits has not been enough to assure the continuation of the breed, which is now on the watchlist.

Disease is the enemy of the stockman. Foot-and-mouth devastated the countryside in 2001. Six million animals were slaughtered in the UK in a bid to stem the virus.

The outbreak of the same disease in 1967 is a faint memory. Whilst local herds escaped the livestock massacre of four hundred and forty thousand, I do remember the fear that penetrated our community. Just as in 2001, foot-and-mouth wiped out bloodstock lines, pedigrees built up over generations, pushing farmers who lived on the red line of bank loans out of business. On this occasion the virus was brought into the country from South America on legally imported lamb. Parents and neighbours talked in hushed undertones, their words taut with worry, and although the disease did not spread to our area, farming is a kinship; what one farmer suffers, all suffer.

WALLS
'too big to be rolled away'[132]

In recent centuries, drystone walls have become so intrinsic a feature in the landscape of the dales that it is easy to forget they are man-made. Most of them date from the Enclosure Acts and were built from the late-18th century onwards. They carry the blood of the dales.

Stone moss home, loom of the dale, limestone grown, millennia of clearings picked from earth, woven into pastures, threading through parishes, stitched into byways, lime kilns, cairns, shelters for sheep, braided into land, like veins on a hand.

Building and repairing these old walls is labour-intensive and a skill that is being lost from the dales as traditional farms decline. As a result, many walls have fallen into disrepair. But in recent decades there has been renewed recognition of their value, both cultural and for the practicalities of the shelter, habitat, and stock control they afford. Their nooks and crannies are a community hub for birds such as great tits and wrens, giving protection to small mammals, including field voles, hedgehogs, common lizards, mice and invertebrates like woodlice, wasps, spiders and beetles; they also support the growth of many species of lichen and mosses. Walls are living architecture, a breathing planet, a safe home.

Government grants are now available for rebuilding and many volunteers give their time and energy to the National Park Authority for the upkeep of the miles of public footpaths and walls that travel the dales.

'Walls are protected.

You must not remove stones.

Use local stone to repair.

Check their condition every year.

Allow the wall to breathe.

Cut back vegetation from their footings.

Prevent tree roots from weakening foundations.'[133]

---

[132] Norman Nicholson, *Wall*.
[133] *Protecting rural landscapes and features*, <https://www.gov.uk/protecting-rural-landscapes-and-features/dry-stone-walls>

Let the walls speak. Sit with your back against their universe, shelter into the textures of lichen: plaster-pinks, rusts, green-grey, gold, cupped, wispy, cauliflowered, needlepoint.

Listen to the creep holes, capstones, through-stones, filling-stones, hearting, stiles and gaps.

As wild as hares, they disappear down gills, chase over moortops, gallop into heather.

Walls are windows, eyes into centuries, herding the wanderers, managing the margins, beginnings and endings.

Stiles in a wall provide a passage through or over, whether they are wooden ladder stiles, a squeeze gap in a wall, or the old, curved iron kissing gates. They represent movement in the landscape, a symbol of an ancient right of way. They are the furniture of a wall, an open door, an invitation to walk forward and travel beyond.

After the Enclosure Act of 1845 and the encroachment of common land, the farming of smaller, walled fields became the foundation of the Yorkshire Dales agricultural economy. Today these walls are mosaics gracing fells alongside stone field barns, known as cow'usses in the local dialect, which are scattered across the landscape, hunkering down into the valley sides as if to protect themselves against the elements. Most of these barns have their origins in the 17th, 18th and 19th centuries, an overcoat of wood and stone, muscle and bone and were built to provide winter shelter for cattle and young sheep, known as hoggs, who were fed the hay that was stored in the mew, or loft space, under the barn's stone tiled roof.

In spring the cattle were let out onto the walled upper pastures to graze, and their muck, which had accumulated over the winter in an outside midden,[134] was then spread onto the lower fields to help the grass grow before the cropping of hay for the following winter. Thus, the barn played a key role in the cycle of the farming year.

This practice continued into the middle of the 20th century when changing farming methods made the barns, and the small farms to which they belonged, largely redundant. Some were converted into dwellings or used as open field shelter for animals in inclement weather, but sadly, many fell into disuse.

---

[134] Midden is derived from the old English word for dung heap.

An abandoned lane on the south side of Swaledale between Gunnerside and Reeth. Notice the old barn is without roof slates. They were probably taken for repairing more functional buildings, leaving the timbers to collapse. The barn is a hollow room open to the unforgiving elements. It will eventually succumb, stone by stone, returning to the sedimentary pulse that throbs below the surface on which it stands.

Below Fremington Edge you surprise, resting in skeletal hawthorns, your roofless shelter abandoned to Swaledale ewes, whilst opportunist alders invade, sap grey once whitewashed walls. Only your boulders talk, scattered and loose-tongued as walkers perch on your foot-worn doorstep, share the eternal scurry of Arkle beck, wonder who once lived, walled into your body.

The Yorkshire Dales National Park now does much to recognise and educate on the social heritage represented by the walls and barns. They are tombs, memorials to farming forebears; the people who crafted a way of life out of these impetuous uplands.

Venture inside the dark chamber of a barn and enter a twilight remnant of the past; wooden cow stalls, earth flooring churned with the dust of decaying animal dung. The smell of mouldy fodder hangs in the air, bird droppings stripe the stone walls as evidence of swallows flown, on the beam cobwebs silver, a barn owl wings-down tight.

The design of the barn, and the traditional dales farmhouse known as a longhouse, is adapted from Norse culture. The field barn is for animal use only, but the longhouse is walled into two separate living spaces: one for the family and one for their animals. Originally, they were built with a cruck-framed roof, comprising of ribs of curved timber thatched over with ling. The pitch was steep, nearly touching the ground on either side, but from the mid-1700s stone slates began to replace thatching which meant the slope of the roof could be reduced and a second storey added. These distinct dwellings remain one of the dominant architectural features in the area and are the hallmark of the hamlets and villages dotted throughout the northern dales as if they have grown from the soil on which they sit.

COMMUNITY
'a parcelling of land for a time'[135]

Every week Mr Pickering's grocery emporium visited our farm and other far-flung holdings in the neighbourhood. The large grey van was packed from floor to ceiling with temptations. Through a door in the side, my mother stepped up to the counter from behind which Mr Pickering served, dressed in a grey flannel shop coat that matched his vehicle.

'Hello there, all okay at Prospect?'

His voice was not as thick with dialect as the families he served. Like my father he was an offcomer to the area, and although both men had lived amongst the villagers for over two decades, they would always be so. An unspoken thread linked those who could count their ancestors as belonging to this corner of Yorkshire; it was an exclusive club.

The weather and illness pre-occupied this shopkeeper, who was never in the best of health himself.

'How are you keepin'?'

'Aye, fair t' middlin' I suppose; as right as can be expected.'

My mother would respond with respectful niceties that pre-empted the more interesting chatter. On this Mr Pickering was never known to disappoint.

'Just heard old Chapman's died.'

'Well, I never.'

This was my mother's typical response to anything that took a few moments to digest.

'It's his birthday next week,' she continued.

'Naye...gettin' older won't bother him now.'

Mr Pickering often sighed to himself as he spoke.

'Mind. He was a bad look for years...only saying to him last week, you look green round the gills, Cecil.'

'Turns out he was worse than we all thought.'

'He'll be worth a few thousand when the will's read.'

---

[135] Marie Bheag, *Dry-stone walling.*

The local paper published the value of estates left by most who had lived in our locality. When the Darlington & Stockton Times arrived each Saturday death announcements and wills were some of the first items to be read. Information gathered would be discussed at auction marts, farmyards or around kitchen tables.

Mr Pickering held an opinion on everyone's business. Sometimes it was good to hang around the van purposefully to overhear the adult gossip. Not only did he transport household goods around the countryside, but births, deaths and scandals were stocked in his shop. He brought the outside world into the homes of farmers who are too busy to engage with anyone other than their immediate neighbours apart from on a market day or at agricultural shows, harvest festivals, winter whist drives and the like. From a child's perspective, he offered the tantalising taste of life beyond the farms.

'Aye…Inquest said young Davey was killed when his tractor rolled over him on South Hill.'[136]

'The village hall's been broken into.'

'And did you know the Rickerby's are movin'?'

'Cricket team lost again last night. Naye…they're a sad lot.'

'Aye…and the bonny young woman that helps out at the Nearly New Shop is pregnant.'

'And her not married. Who's the father I say? Huh?'

'She probably doesn't know herself.'

Womenfolk in our community were the greatest critics of other women. Policing others was structured around tacit rules that had to be abided by if not to fall foul of good opinion.

'You've only got one reputation. Look after it. Once it's lost, it's lost.'

'There are girls, and then there are girls who get themselves into trouble.'

'No one will marry you if you make a name for yourself.'

The exact nature of the demeanours that led to the downfalls was never explained in full. Education was secondary to marriage. I remember asking my mother:

'Why is every song on the radio about love?'

'Because it is.'

The second-wave feminism movement never permeated our home.

---

[136] Before the introduction of rollbars on tractors without cabs, fatal accidents were not uncommon.

All this was a challenge for a young mind and I sailed precariously close to capsizing at times. In sixth form I was exposed to opinions and arguments that contradicted the norms in our community and it became a point of internal friction. I was aware that my brother and the other boys of my acquaintance were not subjected to the same scrutiny as girls. The division of the genders was stark.

'What is the world comin' to?'

This was a question adults often used to ask when the latest ideas infiltrated our community. It was a question that littered everyday observations in what now seems quaint reflection considering the increasingly brutal realities facing the world today. Farming folk are particularly adept at looking backwards to a golden age that masked the hardships and anxieties of their own youth and those before. In the past I have overheard womenfolk talk between themselves about same sex relationships, rape and murder having never happened when they were young.

Until schooldays, Mr Pickering was the only adult I encountered regularly from outside the farming community. His van spilled over with wonders such as *Angel Delight*, *Bird's* custard powder, *Tudor* pickled onion crisps, *Blue Riband* chocolate biscuits, *Ovaltine* bed-time drink, and the Sunday tea-time treat, *Del Monte* tinned peaches. He stocked everything beyond the realms of my father's vegetable garden and the food we produced on the farm, all of which constituted the base for my mother's home-cooking.

When he retired, his van was also pensioned off and my mother shopped in the local village co-operative store, earning dividend stamps through her purchases and collecting them in books that, when full, offered discounts off shopping or payments into a co-op savings account. This shop was the forerunner of the large outlets of today, and whilst the disappearance of Mr Pickering's mobile shop may have passed into folklore, there is a pale reminder in the guise of supermarket time-slotted delivery vans that race around the dale's lanes every day of the year.

Grays, the 'pop' van called in at all the farms now and then. Sometimes we were allowed to buy Dandelion and Burdock because it settled an upset stomach, but Raspberryade - which coloured the skin above our lips bright red - Ice Cream Soda and fluorescent Orangeade were forbidden ket.[137] Even forty years ago, my parents were aware that too many 'E' numbers in luminous fizz

---

[137] A word my father used when referring to anything we consumed that had many artificial ingredients and no nutritional value.

and sweets were not good for children; mother made sure our diet was as free from additives as possible.

My mother also arranged for the mobile library to visit the farm every fortnight. I had already discovered my avarice for books; a trait I inherited from my father. The library was a successor to Mr Pickering. Whilst his wares had stimulated our taste buds, the library put words into our mouths. Now, in an age of instant accessibility to any form of information, there is still huge pleasure in hearing when a rural outpost has created a library, or a book swop in the village pub, a disused red phone box, a bus shelter or within the local shop.

Market day punctuated the week in towns up and down the dales. My father attended Leyburn auction mart most Fridays. It continues to thrive whilst similar small dales market towns, such as Reeth, have seen all retail outlets decline, including the stalls at their Friday market.

Reeth's heyday was in the 18th and 19th centuries when it was a centre for sheep farming, hand-knitting and lead mining. Then, Reeth was a hub for hundreds of lead miners and had many public houses to accommodate the drinking habits of this large workforce. It held six fairs a year and was known to be a place of brawls and drunkenness. The last mine, the CB Mill in Arkengarthdale, closed in 1903 with most of the men having to migrate to the industrial conurbations in County Durham and West Yorkshire to find work. With the end of mining, Swaledale reverted to the pre-industrial agricultural-based economy that my immediate ancestors knew so well.

§

Many local agricultural shows have survived for over a century or more, and still hold a place in the annual social calendar of the dales. Reeth, Muker, Wensleydale, Bowes, Eggleston and Pately Bridge were all shows we regularly attended with our parents to show the Bluefaced Leicesters.

At the end of summer, Reeth Show was the highlight in our farming year. Days beforehand my father dipped, shampooed, trimmed, combed and shined the show sheep to make sure they sported silky white hair on their faces, with bodies of fine curled wool. Developing the quality of the flock was a constant preoccupation amongst my father and his peers and the shows provided a shop window for breeders to exhibit their stock to buyers before the autumn sheep sales.

Adaptations to the most sought-after traits in a Bluefaced Leicester sheep now mean where once white hair on the blue hue of their skin was judged to be the mark of a well-bred animal, today brown or black patches of hair on the face and legs are deliberately bred into show sheep. However, there remains a desire for good bone structure, a distinct Roman nose and large V-shaped ears that stand erect from the head.

Away from the sheep, my mother baked cakes, made lemon curd and selected her best rose for the gent's buttonhole, all to exhibit in the produce tent and be judged by keen-eyed experts. My siblings and I entered the children's classes. We carefully copied out short poems for the best handwriting class, created animals made from vegetables, and planted miniature gardens with twigs and turf on biscuit tin lids.

On the day of the show, we arrived early to a field marked out with the main show ring, exhibition tents and animal pens. The air was full of chatter that tasted of toil and laughter and supportive companionship. Show day was a holiday, a chance to unwind and enjoy meeting the whole community at once.

A tannoy announced timings and triumphs throughout the day. Side stalls lined the perimeter with goods, from horse tack to fudge. A burger van enticed us to peer up into its window as taste buds danced from foot to foot. It was only on a special day such as this that we were allowed smoky hotdogs in soft bread; the ooze of tomato ketchup running through our fingers. It was a banquet.

Around the sheep pens the strong sharp smell of dip permeated the air like a newly tarred road. Farmers and their families gathered in nervous anticipation before the judging began. Young children chased from pen to pen. Older children helped their parents prepare the sheep with one last brush before entering the ring. Here, each animal was encouraged to parade around as one by one the judge signalled to the owners to draw their sheep into a line for the final judging. To be pulled up first was an initial sign of success, but this could be thwarted when the judge made a closer examination of each sheep. The inspection of the wool and the formation of each animal, including what was known in the trade as teeth, tackle and toes, was vital in making the final decision. Sheep were moved up or down the line, depending on the judge's final call. A sigh might permeate the crowd if the first-place sheep was moved down to second before a raised arm meant the judge had made his final decision.

The red, blue, yellow and green rosettes coloured success or emphasised failure as judgements were made class by class. The Show Breed Champion was declared at the end of all the classes and a crescendo of murmurs rose over the pens, clouds of opinions blowing in on gusts of fair or foul.

'Nay, thatun's not a champion, reserve was robbed, t'other divel's a far better yow.'

Or, for the lucky ones, praise was given in scant words.

'Aye, tha's a guddun.'

Then a nod to the economics of a Championship win.

'Tha'll be makin' a packet outa thatun cum sales Robbie.'

Judging in full flow, my father's ewe has been drawn up in line ready for the judge's inspection. It is important that the sheep stands in a position that shows it off to the best advantage: legs square, head up, the bone structure clearly visible.

Focus would then turn to the re-opening of the exhibition tents. Rushing through into the stagnant canvas-air we chased to see if we had any red cards against our entries. To win meant the regal sum of twenty-five pence, a visit to the sweet stall and a happy ride home at the end of the day.

My father standing beside his pen of Bluefaced Leicester sheep at Reeth Show in 1978 with two rosettes tied to the hurdle fence and hopefully more prizes to come.

But this was not before the Fell Races were run, from the starter's gun in the show field to the top of Great Fremington Edge and down again. Although the ascent was four hundred and fifty feet over the two-mile course, it was not about distance or height, but speed and stamina; hardy athletes mirroring the terrain they covered.[138]

Originally the competitors were dales folk, shepherds and miners fit enough from their physical day-to-day work to run without training. Now, members of running clubs from all around Yorkshire, County Durham, Lancashire and beyond take part. The race is recognised as one of the British Open Fell Runner's Association fixtures for the UK Championship, although some races remain exclusively for locals, including those for children and veterans.

At the starting line, vests and muscles, I notice your hair, the colour of limestone, like the black and white photograph of your father, dated 1958. It must be in the genes. You wear the same feet.

---

[138] The current record for the adult race stands at 15 minutes 23 seconds.

The Dales is a television programme fronted by Ade Edmondson which, in 2013, celebrated the centenary of Reeth Show.[139] Watching one evening, a photograph of my father suddenly jumped onto the screen as they chatted about decades of the show.

My father cuts a figure typical of the early fifties, Oxford bag trousers, loose jacket, a soft peaked cap pushed back on his head of dark hair, as it was when he was frustrated; hand in his pocket and his chin sticking out confirms his disgruntlement at the time of this photograph.

The original photograph was not hard to find. Taken in 1952, it portrays a serious looking nineteen-year-old showing a British Friesian heifer. My father recounted that this young animal had already won many prizes, but, as the photograph was being taken, he believed that she had been drawn up last in the line of contenders for the Young Farmer's prize. In fact, after looking at her conformation, the bone structure of her legs, back, chest, her udder, and general condition, she was awarded first prize.

Young Farmers Clubs were an important social adhesion in our community, as they continue to be today.[140] Young Farmers is a large rural-based movement

---

[139] Aired on 3rd June 2013.
[140] The first club was founded in Devon in 1921 to focus on animal husbandry and land management. The National Federation of Young Farmer's Clubs was established in 1932 as membership grew. Run by young people, the movement has developed with the needs of each generation, responsive to their widening interests and concerns within agricultural and rural life.

open to anyone interested in farming and the land. It educates, informs, broadens perspectives, creates opportunities to travel, to debate political and social issues, to learn new skills from ploughing to judging stock to acting in drama competitions and much more. In generations gone by this is where many young people gained their first experience of courting.[141]

Within my grand-parents and parent's group of friends, many farmers' daughters married farmers' sons. In the cluster of farms in our neighbourhood, we had aunties and uncles with no familial relationships other than respect and friendship from their earliest days in Young Farmers.

In our immediate locality none of the wives went out to work off the farm. Their lives were tied to the land in the same way as those of their husbands. Following the tradition of her mother and grandmother before, my mother reared calves, hens, and pet lambs. She helped move stock, deliver eggs, drive tractors, pick potatoes, swill yards and muck out. She cleaned the house, baked, cooked, washed and ironed, spent nights sewing and knitting, brought up children and attended school events on behalf of both parents, all as a matter of routine.

After finishing the outside work for the day, usually with feeding the calves, she would return to the house and change her clothes, from workwear to a dress, before preparing food for teatime. Although there was an equality of work distribution between couples in the farmyard, there remained, within the arena of the farmhouse, a clear distinction between the roles of the sexes.

§

The annual spring-cleaning heralded unwelcome disruption. We returned from school to a home with bare floorboards. Rugs were pulled up and windows yawned, curtain-less and hollow, as blowsy washing blew on lines in the drying green.

'Now you can help by tidying your bedroom drawers. I want all those games you don't play with for the bring-and-buy, and sort through your books, there's far too many to keep.'

'I'm not throwing books out.'

'Well, you can't keep every single one. We're not a library.'

---

[141] A term for dating, used widely at the time by older relatives.

This meant hiding books under the bed in old school bags or piling them up at the back of a bedside cabinet.

Spring cleaning was a curfew on freedom and would mean several days without order; from bedroom ceilings to corners in kitchen cupboards, no part of the house escaped. Tins of paint were opened, the occasional roll of wallpaper pasted onto walls that were scuffed, a new hearth rug might make its way to the fireplace before normality returned.

'Me mother's started cleanin',' was the alarm call we all dreaded.

Once one of the aunties started, the rest followed.

My mother was forever collecting for a bonfire she built on a slab of concrete just inside the field beside the drying green. She would amass redundant cardboard egg trays, orange boxes used to carry groceries home, much thumbed-through dairy cow magazines and Farmer's Guardian newspapers, old work clothes of my father's before he could rescue them, exercise books that had accumulated at the end of a school year, cereal boxes, and general combustible junk. Sometimes we watched from our bedroom window as she poked the flames with a long stick, making them leap above her head before turning her back on the dull ash as the last embers flittered and died.

If her mind weighed heavy with worry, the poker stabbed at the flames, taunting them higher; this would mean keeping out of the way long after she had returned inside.

Red is the colour of beginnings, the dress she wears for their first dance, a song filled with jazz. See it now at the back of her wardrobe hanging amongst her folds of longing. She remembers his jive eyes in every slow walk to the lambing shed, each time she washes the ewes' blood from her hands.

With living and working so closely together, relationships between spouses could become fraught and even the best marriages were put to the test at times. Divorce was unthinkable in our farming circle, and more than one couple tolerated their union rather than expose themselves and their family to the shame of separating.

After the fury, we watch him mend fences; barbed wire, a clawhammer, six-inch nails to fix the smallest gap, the persistent tap-tap as she stands back, bows her head, shrinks into her coat.

Later, silence strangles the kitchen, her eyes the colour of condensation running down the inside of the windowpanes as he sits, throws a hesitant glance, half-minded to read the Farmer's Weekly, half-minded to break down their fences.

One neighbour's wife was an exception to the rest of our aunts. She was given the respectful courtesy of Mrs, even by our parents, as she kept herself a little distant from the chatter of the other women. Older than their neighbours, both husband and wife were given respect, though, on the quiet, he was one of the lads.

Their house was filled with polished mahogany furniture. She had a living room and a best sitting room in which children were forbidden. This set her apart from other homes we frequented. She instilled a little fear and a great deal of respect. She cooked, baked and made jams and chutneys like all the other farm wives, but she did not go outside to work alongside her husband. However, she was active in the Women's Institute, like the other wives, hosting garden parties and events.[142]

§

Every Thursday my mother loaded up the car to deliver eggs on her village round. At each house there was an opportunity to catch up with local news; it was a slow business. As with Mr Pickering's travelling shop, accompanying her on such occasions would mean a great deal of chatter could be overheard if, by perfecting the art of looking distracted, adult tongues slipped their moorings.

Thursday also provided an opportunity to visit Mr and Mrs Atkinson, Uncle Ted and Aunt Maggie, who had moved the mile and a half into Catterick when my father took over the tenancy of the farm in 1960. They lived in the back room of their bungalow, alongside a black cooking range. The oven door yawned with the heat, exposing a cavernous hole from which, on baking day, scones and pies emerged. For Aunt Maggie, the habit of making her own bread continued despite, by this time, the ease of buying a loaf from the village Co-op.

Through the door to a tiny kitchen the dull hum and slosh of a large cream enamelled top loading washing machine, complete with ringers and a barrel-shaped tub, could be heard on washing days. Laundry hung overhead like clouds on a wet day, strung from the ceiling on a dolly maid.[143] Formations of

---

[142] The WI was often a natural progression for girls in Young Farmers after they married.
[143] A wooden slatted pulley clothes airer that was hoisted up close to the ceiling.

tired long johns, bloomers, night shirts, pinnies and numerous collarless shirts, spoke of a different lifetime.

An overriding memory of Uncle Ted is of him sitting in a soft low armchair to the right of the range, his long legs bent at the knees like pyramids making the rest of his body appear small. Beside him was a wooden fixture on the wall that he could easily reach out to whilst seated; this held his grey clay pipes in a row. He continually poked tobacco into one of the pipes, packing it, lighting it, smoking it. This sweet earthy aroma, alongside the trilby hat he wore, even when sat indoors, was a presence, especially next to the diminutive figure of his silver-haired wife. Ted was well-read and talked a great deal of the First World War; established in farming by the outbreak of the Second World War he did not go to fight but contributed with his work on the land.

'Back in the good old days after the Great War, times were lean but we were happy just getting by. Plenty in the cities suffered from no work, but we had it all; hard work was a blessing.'

'Listen to him,' Maggie would interject, 'he wasn't the one carrying water inside in buckets morning, noon and night, nearly breaking his back. No, the horses took care of your heavy work Ted Atkinson.'

He smiled through his pipe smoke, deep in his own reverie.

'All these mod-cons are over-rated, I tell thee. Life was simple then, we were poor, but there would be kith and kin around to help out with the stooking and threshing.[144] All those jobs complicated by machines now.'

'And we knew every soul we came across for miles, and if we didn't, they soon told us their business, no one was a stranger.'

'I think you've got those tinted spectacles on again Ted.'

Listening to him, he taught us the importance of memories, and alongside this, the first inkling that one story could bear many tellings and held many truths.

§

A wooden hut, twice the size of a large domestic greenhouse, stood on our drying green close to the house. The interior was lined in hardboard and

---

[144] Stooking was the gathering of dry hay into bundles in the field. The hay would be hand-forked and brought by cart into stackyards where a hayrick would be built. This was made easier with the invention of the mechanical baler. Threshing machines, originally powered by horses before engines, separated grains of corn from the stalks by a process of beating. They were replaced by the combine harvester.

painted an insipid green. A row of windows graced one side and it sported a proper front door on the end parallel to the eastern gable wall of our house. It had been built for a former tenant of the farm who had been diagnosed with tuberculosis.

Before the middle of the twentieth century, those who suffered from this disease had to be kept from the stuffiness indoors, especially when the fire in the range was stoked and heated for baking and washing days. If not confined to a sanatorium, sufferers would sleep in fresh air, winter and summer alike, under tents, or in a room with the windows wide open.

During the second world war the hut provided accommodation for a labourer, an Italian prisoner of war, who, with a shortage of local men to tend the land, had been enlisted to help on the farm. This former occupant of our playhouse provided much to stoke our imaginations.

'Let's pretend this is a prison cell.'

'I'm going to tie you up so you can't escape.'

Invariably this was the fate of the youngest in our crowd.

At other times the hut became a theatre where we rehearsed plays. My mother had been a keen amateur thespian before her marriage and had plenty of scripts from which we could pretend to create award winning shows.

Alongside our burgeoning acting careers, we had a dressing up box that held old clothes my mother had worn in the 50s and early 60s accompanied by long strings of my grandmother's pearly beads. This was more than enough to dance around fantasising we were Pan's People.[145]

§

In one of my earliest memories I am leaning over a half-filled metal water-trough. My father is leading a young bull by a halter from an old byre out across the stack-yard and up to the trough to drink. The bull nudges my bottom in a playful manner. Already on tiptoes, it takes little to see-saw me into the water. The cold makes me gasp for breath. Rescued, I am carried into the farmhouse and deposited on the clippy rug by the fireside to undress and dry off. I am four years old and have just learnt that although we live side by side

---

[145] An all-girl troupe. They performed dance routines to hits on *Top of the Pops* in the late 60s and early 70s.

with the animals, you can never turn your back on one because they cannot be fully trusted.

We milked the cows in the byre twice daily, morning and evening, all year round. Like schoolchildren, they lined up and filed into their own stalls obediently. Sometimes, if a cow decided not to co-operate and upset the routine, my father's raised voice could be heard interrupting our play, calling us to come and help resolve the stand-off between man and animal.

The cows know time, raise a silent nod to their internal clock, track home and wait, cud-filled at the gate, as though nothing else matters. After milking they scatter, one by one over the pasture, as though the land we share is theirs alone, as though none of this is about us.[146]

The wireless played Radio One during milking. Abba, Dire Straits, 10cc, and many more. The upbeat music helped keep the equilibrium of the parlour in tune with the steady hiss and suck, hiss and suck of the vacuum drawing through the clusters attached to the cows' udders, pulsing the milk along a pipeline into the refrigerated bulk tank in the dairy from which the tanker collected the contents each morning.

Research shows that cows produce more milk when they are played music. The walls rebounded with radio hits from the 60s and 70s. A favourite that resonates with me still was *Born Under a Wand'rin Star*, from the film *Paint Your Wagon*, sung by Lee Marvin in his gravel-mouthed tones. I knew it was a favourite of my father's too. He would turn the volume up so loud when it played, the words carried into the farmhouse:

'*When I get to heaven, tie me to a tree*
Or I'll begin to roam, and soon you know where I will be'[147]

These *wanderin'* words ricocheted inside me with permanency, like the endless pattern of my parents' day-to-day work.

Before the bulk tank heralded change in the early 70s, we filled galvanised cylindrical milk churns and placed them on a milk stand at the farm gate after morning milking for collection by the dairy wagon during the day.[148] The driver picked up the full churns and left empty sterilised ones ready for the evening milking.

---

[146] After *Murmuration*, Katharine Towers, *The Remedies*, Picador: London, 2015, p7, line 9.
[147] Written by Lerner and Loewe, 1951.
[148] Each churn was heavy when filled, holding 50 litres or 11 gallons of milk.

Our cow byres comprised of traditional stalls, originally designed when hand-milking was the mode; here two cows stood side by side in one concrete bay. Creatures of habit, each cow would know to stand in their own stall, although occasionally my father had to move some cows around if they began to argue with each other.[149] He then placed a loose chain around their necks to stop them going walkabout. Every stall had a small trough in which feed was measured and then slices of baled hay were dropped into ricks attached to the wall just above their heads. Long pink tongues would reach for the fodder, chewing the winter hours away: in summer all cattle were out in the fields on grass, both day and night.

In the byres, a long concrete channel ran just behind the cows' back legs to catch the muck and pee. Twice daily it would be manually scrapped clean with a shovel and thrown into a small wheelbarrow, then wheeled out to the muck heap where the contents were deposited.[150] After swilling and brushing the byres down, the cows were given a fresh bed of straw. These labour-intensive stalls were substituted for loose housing as herd sizes grew, milking parlours were introduced and old-fashioned byres became redundant.

Scraping out the muck and feeding-up became the work of one man and his tractor. Now much of the manual work has been replaced by computerised systems and zero grazing where cows are kept inside throughout the year and fed cut grass, silage and high protein cattle-feed.[151]

We sold our milk to the Milk Marketing Board; a farmer owned co-operative formed for the countrywide control of milk production and distribution.[152] My father was a registered producer and was paid on the quantity and quality of the milk that was collected daily. When bulk tanks were substituted for churns, the tankers picked the milk up from the many small dairy farms on their daily route before returning to the depot in Northallerton; a subsidiary company of the MMB, called Dairy Crest, was responsible for the pasteurising and bottling of the doorstep milk on into the food industry.

Today, the cattle we live alongside are more than two thousand generations removed from their original wild ancestors and relatively domesticated. Our

---

[149] Like all animals, cows have individual likes and dislikes which include other cows and humans.
[150] This was a weekend job where I earned the royal sum of £16 for one winter's work when I was in my early teens.
[151] One advantage of zero grazing is the ability to feed clean cut grass efficiently which is thought to promote higher levels of milk production. It helps with land management and consequently is a cheaper source of food. A disadvantage is that dairy cattle can become stressed if their movements are continually confined.
[152] Established by the Agricultural Marketing Act, 1933.

pedigree herd comprised of cows that carried their mother's name, indicating their birth line, each subsequent female calf thereafter being numbered chronologically.[153]

There was only a handful of names amongst the cows: Isabell, Buttercup, Dairymaid, Jenny, Dainty, Joyce. Some maternal lines multiplied and produced many heifer calves, Isabelle's beyond the 47th, Joyce, the 41st. Bulls that were kept for breeding were also given the prefix: Ricdon Nulty, Ricdon Ranunculus, Ricdon Vanguard. Ricdon Elizabeth 1st was my father's favourite cow. As her name suggested, she reigned supreme, her calves were prized, her milk yield praised. No cow matched this bony, ungainly matriarch of the Ricdon herd who was reprieved from being sent to the market geld when she grew older. Instead, she lived out her days alongside the productive youngsters that continually kept the farm viable.

Mr Leeming visited monthly to record the yield and quality of our milk on behalf of the MMB. He carried a much-used, small wooden box with leather handles which was compartmentalised to hold tiny, sterilised bottles with orange screw tops.

'What are you doing now?'

We gathered around him with our noses in the box.

'Same as last month, taking a drop of milk from every cow, then I'll send it to the lab to get tested.'[154]

He wrote each cow's registered number on a clean bottle, carefully returning it to the box when the sample had been collected.

'When we post your Dad the results he can tweak the herd, so hopefully any improvements will mean more profit.'

He winks at father.

'Then you might get that pony you mither[155] about.'

Mr Leeming was a small man who wore a tan coloured overall to protect his clothing from the watery sprays of cow-shit that, at any time and without warning, hit the back walls of the byres and all who were in the way. There was laughter and entertainment when anyone got a splattering. His presence was a diversion from getting under our mother's feet, so we lingered in the byres

---

[153] Male calves were sold when they were young. They would be bought to rear and fatten for the meat market. As I grew up, I sometimes found the practicalities of farming distressing.
[154] Milk was tested for butterfat content, protein, mastitis pathogens, bacteria and added water.
[155] Nag or make a fuss.

watching him at work. A man on the farm with a pen in his hand was an intriguing sight.

Pedigree heifer calves born on the farm had to have their distinct black and white markings recorded and sent to the British Friesian Cattle Society as validation of the lineage and identity of each animal. On pre-printed outlines of a calf's body, my father would meticulously draw their markings in pencil. Then, with ink pot and pen he painted in the black features of each new-born. Sitting bowed over his desk, he sketched with the same precision as that of an architect. These were the days of labour-intensive work before technology intervened. Current practice is to issue calves with electronically chipped ear tags that incorporate their DNA analysis and a passport, by which their every movement is tracked and recorded.

Cows, like dogs and all farm animals, have a connection with their humans, and possess their own characters. Some are leaders, some followers. Some attached themselves to my father and jealously head-butted other cows that sought his attention. These stalkers would swish their tails, vying with others as they followed him when he walked the herd. Some cows would kick off the cups on their teats when they were being milked; in summer flies could be troublesome, but often it was ill-temper.

'Just for th' divelment,' my father would complain.

Some cows were good milkers, some not so; some had an uncanny knack of producing a heifer annually, others frustrated with bull calves far too often.

To keep the dairy stock at its optimum the herd had to produce the next generation with consistency. We would watch out for signs of cows ready to serve as they climbed on top of each other, then hurry and tell father.

All our bulls were carefully bred for their bloodlines. When the ladies were first introduced to one of these youngsters, he showed no interest at all. His attitude became the subject of conversations with neighbours who would lean over the door of his pen to give their verdict on this unusual behaviour.

'Ee's a fine specimen Robbie, there's no doubt about that.'

'What the flamin' heck is it then?'

'He's equipped for the job, more than capable I'd say.'

'There's something wrong. Something funny.'

'Aye. Remember a bad on' costs as much to feed as a good on'.'

My father's cap would be pushed back as he scratched his head with frustration.

'He's just not interested in the women.'

'Well, I think you'll have to fetch the AI man. These lasses aren't going to get themselves in calf.'

§

Our small, registered flock of Bluefaced Leicester sheep was kept for the purpose of breeding superior tup lambs. Each year we retained the best of our gimmers to replace older ewes, but the focus was on selection within the male line to produce prize winning tups that would be sold at the autumn sheep and sales in Hawes, Hexham, Carlisle and Kelso. Here, shepherds from all over the country would gather throughout the September sales season in search of pure breeding stocks and rams to cross with Swaledale ewes to produce the Mule lamb.

A tup that won the 'best in show' award preceding the sales added much value to himself and left more than a little sense of pride for the breeder, who, with the revenue from his sales, could then afford to buy-in top class animals carrying the genes he required to further improve his flock.

The breeding of Leicesters was a religion amongst my father and his like-minded peers, and the selection and purchase of a champion tup involved a considerable amount of time, worry and expense.

My father and uncle in Northumberland clubbed together to purchase one such animal, with much expected of him later that autumn when he was released with the ewes to do his work. Subsequently, Sunday nights were passed in optimistic conversation over the telephone concerning the forthcoming performance of this male specimen.

Unfortunately, he was not to reward the trust placed in him. The greener pastures in the sky beckoned, and he succumbed. A fatal blow to both bank balances and hopes.

'Every sheep dreams of dyin'.'

This unhelpful observation came from an elderly Northumbrian farming friend. From his experience, my father maintained sheep gave up on life too easily. To rear any flock is never anything less than challenging and on occasions confirmed that in farming nothing except mortality can be taken for granted.

When I ask for a memory, you give me the dead ewe beside a drystone wall. She had fought her afternoon heaving against a birth your knife brought swiftly. The new-born gimmer so large, dressed blue in afterbirth beside her mother, their wool the colour of tombstones.

We are constantly reminded we share our environment with huge personalities who are not exclusively human. Occasionally on walks with the dogs we come across a ewe who stands her ground, stamping her front feet in defiance at our intrusion. Once, to my surprise, a lone sheep charged at us and before I could react, she had circumnavigated me to head-butt the first dog she could reach. She then shot off into the field in triumph; this small round ball of shaggy wool was boss and she knew it. One encounter was enough for the dogs to learn to give all ewes and lambs a wide berth.

During the summer when the sucklers[156] are on the moor above Downholme, there are frequent stand-offs between cars, cyclists and cattle on the road leading out of the village. As if deliberately, the herd often stands chewing their cud by the cattle grid or in the middle of the road, without any intention of moving for car horns, shouts and waving arms. Here, man and beast can happily inhabit the same environment as equals.

At midnight, on a lonely, wooded dales road I come across an adult buck standing astride the middle white line. Obstinate, and not in the mood to move for me, I must stop the car. He stares directly into my headlights, asserting himself with stubborn fortitude like a belligerent teenager. I am alone and decide to slowly drive around him rather than get out of the car and try and move him. The next morning, I return past the spot where I encountered him. In the weak winter daylight, he ghosts the road.

---

[156] A cow that is used to breed and suckle calves that are reared for beef.

CUSTOMS
'these knots of life are everywhere'[157]

In Swaledale, high up Swinnergill, just west of Muker, a gorge widens at a waterfall where a cave known as Swinnergill Kirk lies hidden high in the strata of rocks. Here, during the 1600s, Catholics secretly gathered to pray; driven into the shadows by the fear of being persecuted by the Protestant majority. They would post a lookout to watch over the fell and protect the worshippers who would retreat deep into the cave if warnings were given. In this haven of nature and geology, politics and religion trespassed.

In the 1760s, John Wesley's concern for the souls of miners and the poor brought him and his followers north to preach their evangelical philosophy of compassion for the lower classes.[158] By the end of his life Wesleyan Chapels had been established in many villages and hamlets strung across the dales. These buildings, few of which still exist as places of worship, stand testament to the size of the population that lived and were employed in the area before the lead mining industry declined. Most chapels are now converted into homes and business premises but still bear witness to the influence religion had over generations of working people.

Although some elders of my youth refused to carry out tasks such as cutting grass or baling hay on the Sabbath, as old farmers have died so have these old ways. Few farmers can afford not to work if the sun is shining on a Sunday.

Like so many farming families in the north of England, my mother was brought up in the Methodist tradition, observing an abstinence from alcohol and a dislike of excess in general. Public houses met with disapproval; they were responsible for the serious undoing of righteous, hardworking folk and were out of bounds to anyone wishing to avoid damnation. The only exception she made to this rule appeared to be a neighbouring farmer who managed to indulge a love of real ale whilst keeping his reputation intact.

§

---

[157] Nan Shepherd *The Living Mountain*.
[158] A blue plaque in Newbiggin, Richmond, marks the steps where Wesley once preached his philosophy; that every life, no matter how poor, was equal in front of God.

At thirty metres, Hardraw Force in Wensleydale is the highest single drop waterfall above ground in England. It is encased within the bowl of limestone that is Hardraw Scar and entering it, as a child, was like venturing into middle earth.[159]

The only access to the fall is through the Green Dragon public house in the village of Hardraw, and when we were young provided an opportunity to set foot in such a place. It was a mysterious den.

'Where does the dragon live?'

'It must be close by, it stinks!'

'It smells more like the calf house.'

'And that fire's just like Aunt Maggie's.'

A large fire roared up a wide stone chimney breast. Beside it, on the wall, hung brightly polished horse brasses on leather straps just like my grandfather's. However, it was the large worn wooden-framed bar and the array of men slouched against it that fascinated me. Flat tweed caps were pulled well down into ruddy weathered faces as heads huddled together, each man holding a pewter tankard in their rough, worn hands. I stared, eager to see what a man on the path to ruin looked like. But we were hurried through by our mother to wait in the beer garden at the back whilst my father bought tickets to visit the waterfall.

The eternal fall of Hardraw beck sings with the water-music of this upland landscape, and on summer Sundays the sound of brass can be heard resounding off the open limestone auditorium of the scar. Catch a concert and you will hear how the music reflects the character of the dale and its people; unpretentious, bold, harmonious.[160]

§

In a pub near Reeth, musicians gather every Thursday evening. They bring along guitars, cellos and violins. The music is impromptu and is dependent on which musicians attend. The sounds of folk and jazz merge easily into each other. There are spontaneous outbursts of singing, stamping of feet and clapping to the beat. On a winter's night, beside the open fire, with curtains closed tight to the inclement weather, their tuneful arrangements spill out

---

[159] Reference to Norse mythology and J.R.R. Tolkien's imagined world in *The Lord of the Rings*.
[160] The first brass band festival at Hardraw was held in 1881.

through the door whenever it is opened, into the darkness, over fells, mingling with the wandering minstrels of centuries past.

My parents' generation, and generations before them, enjoyed Old Time dancing. Held in one of the local village halls on a Saturday night, the band played accordion, drums and fiddle whilst the assembled company partnered up to dance sequences such as the Dashing White Sergeant, the Military Two Step and the Gay Gordons; folk names that have all but vanished. In my last year at primary school the headmaster's wife taught the girls to dance the maypole. In pagan custom the maypole represents the tree of life.[161] The dance symbolises fertility and is a celebration of the return to the warmth of the growing season.

The boys performed a sword dance, with long wooden blades. This dance, with origins in the north of England, honoured the earth in anticipation of a successful harvest to come. We danced in front of parents and dignitaries at Speech Day in July. It felt like a ritualistic passing through into new beginnings which spoke of possibilities and hope. The final dance, Strip the Willow, included both boys and girls together, our young bodies weaving in and out of each other's steps in dizzying circles, girls wearing beaded headdresses and black skirts trimmed with bright, colourful ribbons, the boys in breeches gathered at their knees. A fitting finale to the first years of childhood before heading up into big school.

In the early 1970s few youngsters were still being taught these old rituals and for a time, before our teens, discos, and later, clubs, we relished being allowed to attend dances with our parents on special occasions. The village hall would throb to the sound of feet and heave with laden tables of supper, all the womenfolk having offered a cake or sandwiches towards the feast. A tee-total event, the infectious and innocent merriment was an interlude for my parents from the harsh reality of their day to day worries and work.

During our primary school years, we made corn dollies in the autumn term, another symbol of our pagan past. Patiently, we plaited long stems of straw and wove them into shapes to thank Mother Earth for the harvest just gathered in. Skilful hands could produce intricate three-dimensional figures, but ours were simple hollow twisted prisms. At home, we would hang them on a nail in the wall by the back door. Historically they were buried in the fields during seed planting the following spring to bring good luck and abundance in the new growing season.

---

[161] Norse mythology told of a world tree at the centre of the cosmos known as Yggdrasil.

Every Christmas Eve the old ways still gallop into Richmond marketplace in the shape of the Poor Owd 'Oss. Its origins are unclear but rooted in pre-Christian culture. The 'oss was once a genuine horse's skull covered in material, with wild white eyeballs and a full mouth of teeth. It is carried on a pole by one of the mummers with another person stooped behind them like a pantomime horse.[162]

Traditionally, the body was covered with a horse pelt, but today this is substituted by a modest dark-brown blanket. The horse's mouth, puppet-like, mimes out the drama. Mummers and musicians carry squeeze boxes.[163] Clad in red huntsmen's coats, bright waistcoats and berried crowns, they accompany the 'oss like sprites spirited from the winter solstices of a distant past, their black top hats encircled with sprigs of holly and ivy. As the performance progresses, the virile young horse eventually slows with age until death overcomes the poor animal. It falls to the floor only to be revived by a loud blast from a hunting horn. The horse rises once more re-joining the chorus celebrating the cycle of birth and renewal.

Like the Morris and maypole dancers of early summer, the merrymaking and frivolity of the mummers is a celebration of mid-winter, acted out with the same vitality as their sun-loving counterparts.

In the days before Christmas the 'oss and mummers visit the pubs in the dales, singing Christmas Carols with enough vigour to wake the ghosts of Christmas past which haunt many of these old hostelries. The 'oss lives on the cusp between a living heritage and vanishing customs.

§

My mother's home-cooking followed the seasons and our diet remained much the same as it had been for our grandparents and great-grandparents, based on recipes passed on from one generation into the next. Our food was simple, fresh and wholesome. The carb-based fayre filled the bellies of hard-working folk; meat, plenty of potatoes and bread and butter, formed the basic meal, with a pudding to follow.

One of Yorkshire's most famous delicacies is the Yorkshire pudding, which in a true Yorkshire custom is eaten before the main Sunday roast dinner with a

---

[162] A troupe of amateur actors.
[163] A hand-held box shaped instrument with bellows that squeeze in and draw out to make musical notes.

lettuce and spring onion salad, known as wet salad by some.[164] Yorkshire puddings are made from cheaper cupboard ingredients - flour, eggs and milk - and were originally designed to take the edge off big appetites before the main meal, so that less meat would be eaten.

'Who eats a pudding with gravy and lettuce.'

My Northumbrian relatives laughed when I realised for the first time that even within farming communities things could be done differently.

Now, as then, Yorkshire has a superb selection of artisan cheese makers. These skills can be traced back to the Roman occupation and the influence of French monks who settled in the region after the Norman invasion. Yorkshire monasteries, such as Jervaulx and Fountains, farmed considerable numbers of sheep, producing ewes-milk cheese in quantity. Prior to their dissolution and disbanding, the monks shared recipes with the local farming communities that remain the basis for the cows, sheep and goats milk cheeses produced today.

The abbeys and dales lend their names to the cheeses made within their locality. Wensleydale cheese has Protected Geographical Indication Certification[165] which means all the cheese sold under the name Yorkshire Wensleydale is produced in the dale. The creamery at Hawes is a major tourist attraction in the area and far removed from the dark, cool cellars of old farmhouses, furnished with stone-slab shelves for maturing young cheeses that was the centuries old method of production. Wooden butter presses, barrel churns, cheese moulds and other cheese-making and dairy equipment used to be widely available at local farm clearances. Now they are displayed in folk museums like those in Hawes and Reeth.

My mother would occasionally make creamy butter during the summer months when grass was lush and plentiful, and there were plenty of newly calved cows with milk that had a high fat content; but the process was labour intensive and could not compete with the convenience of mass-produced butter.

In the days before refrigeration, milk that was surplus to daily requirement was preserved as butter or cheese, and cheese became a staple food for the army of men who worked in the fields. The ploughman's lunch was convenient and hearty food for farm labourers. Recipes and methods for cheese-making varied from farm to farm, passing through generations of families, often by word of

---

[164] The recipe I inherited for Yorkshire salad is a combination of lettuce, spring onions, fresh mint, white wine vinegar and a little dash of cream, all seasoned with freshly ground black pepper.

[165] Awarded by the EU in 2013, it protects the name of Yorkshire Wensleydale as cheese produced exclusively in Wensleydale. Formerly made with ewes' milk, this crumbly, mild cheese with a slightly acidic texture and taste, is now made with cow's milk.

mouth, making each producer's cheese distinctive and unique. The skimmed milk and whey left as a by-product would be fed to young calves and pigs reared on the farm.

Recently, small artisan cheese and ice cream makers can be found once again in the dales. Old skills are being reinstated as a way of future-proofing some contemporary rural businesses. Cheese-making has seen a revival as part of the sustainable food movement. Farmers' markets now help to promote seasonal food and, in the dales, independently owned supermarkets sell a feast of local artisan produce. Allotments are increasingly sought after, and many people are revisiting, or becoming acquainted with, a vegetable patch and home-produced food. This is not harking backwards but projecting forward into safer foods produced on our doorsteps, eliminating the climate impact of food-miles.

My father produced honey from his own bees. A local beekeeper, an apiarist rather than a hobbyist as my father was, also had hives on our land. Our bees were common honeybees, but his were Italian and very cantankerous. We would give them a wide berth whenever we walked close by their hives.

In the summer, my father loaded his hives onto a trailer and we took them up onto the moor near Leyburn until September. Here, these tiny dynamic machines produced the deep golden sweetness of heather honey. The hives were returned home in early autumn and we would watch as my father carefully removed the wooden frames from them.

'Why do the bees make hexagonal combs?'

'Because they fit together perfectly, if they were circles, they wouldn't.'

'How do they know that?'

'Nature is very clever. Much wiser than us sometimes.'

He would then cut the wax off the surface of the comb with a hot knife releasing the honey to drip down into a container.[166]

'A drop of summer to spread on your toast in winter.'

'An' don't forget we can't take it all. The bees need some honey for themselves too.'

Beekeeping in the UK stretches back thousands of years, but we had no need of a book to tell us this. The history and the mechanics of making honey were a story that ran through childhood, every year another chapter in our understanding.

---

[166] Known as uncapping.

TIME

'if we do not preserve the poetry of history, it will cease to exist'[167]

In Reeth I meet Carol Drinkwater, an actor who used to star in the 1970s TV series *All Creatures Great and Small*.[168] She is revisiting old filming haunts for a newspaper article. She reminisces that Swaledale is unchanged in the forty years since her last visit. In many ways she is right. The surface rock that makes up the dales landscape we see today is around 300 million years old and until the last few centuries, with the pursuit of forest clearing, mining and sheep farming, change has been barely perceptible. But ask a local what they think about the conversion of the old butcher's shop into a house, new owners taking over an established business in the town, or the death of a local stalwart and they will tell you these are the events that herald real change.

I also meet two men who, in their time, have played their own role in the evolution of the dale. The first man worked for the North-Eastern Electricity Board in the 1960s and was part of the team that brought electricity to the last twelve farms at the top of the dale near Muker and Keld. What a difference being connected to the grid must have made to these remote dwellings. There are locals from these communities who still remember carrying water into their homes collected in water-barrows from streams and wells. Bathrooms, washing machines and lightbulbs came late to remote farmsteads.

The second gentleman had a long family association with Reeth. But he was equally proud that his father founded a store in a local market town selling electrical appliances when electricity was first introduced into the lower dales in the 1940s. This business still thrives.

§

There are days that haunt; days that linger from childhood. Each year we moved a group of heifers about three and a half miles along public roads between Snape and Masham onto summer grazing. Hedgerows abundant with yarrow, wild basil, rough meadow grass and common bent spilled scents of

---

[167] Stig Abell, *The Independent*, 19th April 2019.
[168] A tv programme made from the books written by the vet James Herriot, who practised in Yorkshire from 1939 for 50 years.

June into the lanes. We were drovers, Gabriel Oak[169] travelling alongside us. Driving unbiddable young animals was fraught with dashing backwards and forwards to keep them moving, slowing oncoming traffic, hurrying the stragglers, diving into open gateways to prevent an invasion of hooves over pristine lawns and gardens. We could taste the salt of our sweat; our jumpers tied at our waists, trailing down over the tops of our wellies.

'Get by,' we whistled and shouted waving our arms, outrunning the young animals until finally they were safe in our fields that overlooked the rooftops of Masham.

'That's a canny day's work. Now then, who's for a 99?'

'Meee!' We replied in a chorus.

The menfolk never failed to reward our help with sugar. We would make our way into the town square and sit, fathers and youngsters, in silent companionship eating soft cold Mr Whippy ice-cream from a local café.

'Reckon we all deserve this.'

My father would observe quietly as he pushed his cap back off his brow.

§

It now seems a privilege to have experienced a protected childhood in the manner of our little enclave of Yorkshire, but for most families modernity could not be kept at bay.

Many children, including my brother, decided they did not want to farm, and so the traditional line of succession on farms in our neighbourhood dwindled, assigning a way of life to the archives. For my brother, the challenges of long hours of work for a relatively low income compared unfavourably to the balanced lifestyle of his contemporaries in industries that offered higher wages and the freedom of weekends. Reluctantly, he made the decision to leave farming and attend agricultural college to study turf science and sports ground management, eventually setting up his own business in maintaining green spaces from golf courses to gardens.

'Farming's in the blood.'

How often when I was young was this saying repeated? But passion does not generate enough to make a living. Like all industries, farming requires

---

[169] Thomas Hardy's shepherd in *Far from the Madding Crowd*.

adaptation, diversification and money. As farms were given up by ageing tenants without a successor, their land was distributed amongst those that remained under the council ownership allowing for greater viability, and so one less farm, one less farmer, one less family continued in the footsteps of tradition. The policy on council farms changed in the early years of the twenty-first century and they were sold off as tenancies ended. In our community only one or two remain as working farms.

Towards the end of the last century, as farming practices advanced, the number of hands needed on farms went into decline. Increasing mechanisation and economic factors have meant that smaller farms do not have the work for a son or daughter alongside their father, as happened in the decades before.[170] This has precipitated the increasing number of children who work away from the land, some not returning to take over the family farm when parents reach retirement.[171] As a result, the average age of a farmer has steadily increased.[172] The shortage of young blood feeding in at the bottom of the industry has contributed to the reduction in the natural passing on of knowledge accumulated over centuries. Some may say that the impact of this is minimal as skills evolve with the times, but intrinsic knowledge of land and animal welfare is a constant in farming. Food security is now of greater concern than ever as we move further into this century. Who is going to continue to grow our food if agriculture does not attract the farmers of tomorrow?

Intensive farming now dominates many agricultural practices beyond the dales. Farming philosophy is often dictated by supermarkets as they have emerged as one of the greatest economic influences on the industry. Contract farming is the way forward for many farms, including those owned by my relatives. Embracing biotechnology is to be commended.[173] Farming is no longer a matter of good or bad luck discussed over a neighbour's gate but the business of risk mitigation and profit margins planned out in boardrooms, laboratories and farm offices.

---

[170] In reality, on remote dales farms the makeshift roads to the farm were prohibitive to the larger milk tankers, and with no means to upgrade these private roads, sadly the decision had to be made to cease dairy farming.

[171] Young people outside of agriculture can find it almost impossible to start up in farming; cost being the biggest barrier. There are avenues such as crowdfunding, taking on a tenancy, apprenticeships, training programmes, but as it was in my father's day, and so it remains, a tough process that requires huge commitment and a little good fortune.

[172] In 2021 the average age of a farmer is 59 years; in the 1978 it was 50 years.

[173] The term covers a wide definition, but to oversimplify, it is technology based on biology and used in agriculture to protect crops and animals from diseases, obtain greater yields, and to increase the quality and nutritional value of food.

However, despite scientific advancements, the public are becoming increasingly conscious of where and how their food is being produced. Food miles, climate change, animal sentience, disease control, genetic modification, pesticides, veganism and the threat to rare breeds, are all factors that cannot be separated from the economics of how food is farmed. The present revolution in farming is only in its infancy. As with the motor industry, consumers will determine the future as we continue to become more conscious of our moral responsibilities to the planet and the generations that follow.

The economic benefit of industrial farming narrows the viability for smaller producers even further. Are those that make the most money from farming the best managers of our land? The move towards re-wilding may mean farmers evolve into custodians of land rather than food producers. As fewer businesses become responsible for producing greater quantities of food, will we see them further detached from the essence of farming as we know it? Or is the will to farm and buy seasonal fresh food within the locality it is produced a movement that will continue to gain momentum with the public?

At present, the answers lie in the economic decisions made by the largest buyers, the supermarkets. Extenuating circumstances, such as the pandemic, has seen the growth in local markets and in the footfall in marketplaces in the dales. But whilst the answers do not lie in a return to a little country, we do have the gift of hindsight to choose what we take forward from historical knowledge for the benefit of both humans and the natural world. Juggling sustainable nutritious food production within the parameters of an economically viable profession, whilst protecting the environment, is the foremost focus for farmers today. Agriculturalists and farmers must leave a healthy industry for the next generation to give them a fighting chance when they pick up the baton and face their own challenges. This is not a new lesson but stretches right the way back to the Anglo-Saxons and before.

FAREWELL
'pack up the moon and dismantle the sun'[174]

Some farms still have a redundant milk-stand at their farm gate long after the farm has been subsumed into a neighbouring farm or development, especially if they have been built of stone. Each monument tracks a history and those who travel the maze of rural roads in the northern dales can bear witness to long lost farming communities through such signifiers.

One of the most harrowing times for a farmer comes with the realisation that although the head will always farm, the body, often the lungs, can no longer continue.[175] If there is no one to pass the farm down to, the farm sale becomes an inevitable reality. The breaking up and dispersal of a lifetime of arduous work, of years taken up with building blood stocks, of the habit and repetition of seasonal patterns that trick us all into believing in forever, can be debilitating. There is no preparation for the severing of a farmer from his farming life. It is an amputation.

After a sleepless night, he meets your bovine heavy eyes, greets you one last time. Only your blood warms him, threads the past, weaves through his veins like a country without borders. You have walked the mornings together so long, the land is your heart; the land is your feet, the land is your tongue, the land hears the last echo of the gavel, the last cattle wagon door drawn up, watches the last stranger leave the farm, tells of the last morning and mourns deeply under red skies.
Empty of you, he closes the gate on a lifetime.

When the stock is sold, the unravelling of a farm culminates in the sale of the machinery and, on occasions, the contents of the house. Saturday afternoons often offered a chance to lay down the work on our own farms and attend a farm dispersal sale. Here, stepping-stones of a life, the story of a family, were placed in the field next to the farmhouse for strangers' eyes to look over and evaluate their worth; brown furniture that had passed through the hands of mothers, daughters, fathers, sons. The farmer and his wife would watch on as their possessions transferred into the hands of strangers, lot by lot.

---

[174] W H Auden, *Twelve Songs*, IX.
[175] Farmer's lung disease is caused by the mould dust off hay and grains causing inflammation in the lungs and resulting in difficulty breathing. It was a common illness in older farmers when I was young.

'A fine dresser, solid and still a useful bit of furniture. Come on don't be shy, I'm sure there's a buyer amongst you. Where shall we start?'

Each bid was like an axe to a tree.

'Is that the final offer? Going once, going twice, sold to the gentleman in the tweed jacket at the back.'

Knocked down on a small wooden block, the gavel reverberated over corrugated tin roofs, the old Dutch barn, the milking parlour, calf houses, lambing sheds and the ghosts of all the families that had once called this land their home.

In hapless order, lots strung like underwear on a washing line. An eavesdropping of kilner jars, jam pans, horse brasses, billy cans, a family Bible faithfully scribed in tarnished gold, Births Marriages Deaths sinewed into leather. Passed on, passed by, faded names and dead men's dates. Last entry, a family epitaph.

'What am I bid?'

Our own farm sale took weeks of planning. It involved every item of machinery and small tools, all the large animals except a few sheep which my father was taking with him to the field my parents had bought and built a bungalow on; everything else that had been gathered over the decades was to be sold. Auctioneers were booked, catalogues printed; each pedigree cow, heifer and calf given a lot number, as were all the miscellaneous goods, even down to the last bundle of fencing posts. Lastly, the farm itself was buffed and brushed tidy.

The day before the sale, many hands helped as straw bales were set out in a circle to make an auction ring with stairs of bales set-up as seating in the Dutch barn. Parking was organised in a field that was conveniently close to the farmstead. The field with the hollowed ash tree was used to lay out the working items to be auctioned: the tractor, trailers, muck spreader, hedge-cutter, fertiliser spreader, ladders, an electric generator, calf pens, an assortment of ropes, a dog kennel, the medicine chest that belonged to Mr Atkinson, the old Avery weighing scales that had stood in the barn since before my father arrived as a youngster.

On a warm, fine July day my father woke thankful the weather was kind enough to encourage the turnout needed to reap a decent profit from the sale. Friends, farmers and dealers filled both stackyards; men, women and children. Pedigree cattle attracted buyers from far and wide. The younger relatives from Northumberland had arrived the night before and started washing the stock at dawn so all the cows and heifers looked their best by noon, ready for the sale ring. Interested parties arrived early to gather in the byres, marking their catalogues against the lots they would bid for.

Preparing the cows for the sale ring.

Homemade refreshments were served in the small back yard outside our kitchen door. A large water boiler had been brought in to keep up with teas and coffees. But when the auction was about to start, all stations were abandoned and everyone crowded into the upper stackyard.

I sit alone, high on a stack of bales, watching the scene below as if opening a window onto a circus, surrounded by chatter, the rhythm and patter of the auctioneer in a rise and fall of song. The air is overwhelmed with the stench of fear drifting above bewildered cattle. Their panic palpable, as one by one they are encouraged into a slow circular walk around the makeshift ring. I wonder where the clowns are, the trapeze artists, wish it were only a show.

'Lot 34. A fine heifer, good-looking beast, calved 2 weeks ago, you've got all the information in front of you...So, who's going to start me off...'

The auctioneer is the shepherd of the sale, rounding up buyers, steadily gathering the bids, keeping a discreet nod in his line of sight, shutting the gate swiftly when the highest offer is attained. Importantly, an experienced auctioneer knows the value of what they are selling, the prices to expect, and if certain buyers are in the crowd, which lots can be pushed higher.

I watch the spectacle with the weight of inevitability. It is like peeling back skin, exposing every organ that has pumped with the blood of Prospect Farm. This has been my parents' little country for forty years.

The auctioneer taking bids whilst my father stands beside him deep in thought.

A sudden realisation washes up through my body: when everything is stripped and sold, we will leave behind the purple lilac between the garden and the drying green; the apple tree my sister planted from a pip; the knotted roots of a horse chestnut where, when I was fourteen, I fell off my pony on Father's Day and knocked myself unconscious; the grave of our beloved dog Lassie. This eclectic mix of memories has made this farm a home. I watch my parents;

farmers afford little time for sentimentality. They appear pragmatic, getting on with the business of the day, but later my mother voices her thoughts when we sit, emptied of the day.

'Thank goodness that is over', and then, to herself, 'even if it feels as if we've cut every rope that has tethered us here.'

Today, if you drive along Tunstall Road where our community once laboured, reared beef, sheep and pigs, milked cows, grew turnips, mangolds and potatoes, barley and beet, worked hard and long hours in the days when loan interest rates were 15% or more, you will see affluently populated barn conversions, holiday lets and businesses.

However, the original footings of the byres, barns and dairies on these farmsteads can still be traced by the informed eye. Years later, when I return to Prospect Farm, I am tinged with loss at the demise of a way of life small farms once supported. We embrace the future for our children and grandchildren, but also hope that they will understand something of their heritage. That around the country the memory of small farming communities will continue to be remembered with affection and respect.

LEGACY
'Not one of us will live forever - the world is far too beautiful for that'[176]

I purchase a notebook. Just as a child does, I turn to the first page and write the title at the top: *Privilege*. This is the first sensation that percolates my senses when looking back at Prospect Farm. I begin to touch, smell, hear a life across the decades, recalling the many people who once populated our little country and have now sadly passed. But what they have left behind is the certainty and understanding that something was once special, and the essence of it is worth preserving.

As I begin to write, some memories show themselves immediately; some are more reticent, and some will be for others to find years later. Even now, few remember the womenfolk sat in front of farmhouse ranges on winter nights cutting up old cloth to make rag rugs. But these simple acts tell much of life. How else do we recognise ourselves if we do not understand that it is the ordinary stitches of the present that will become the embroidery of social history. I have waited patiently for each detail I have written, and each recollection, in its turn, has found me.

The dales are like parents, encouraging independence, without relinquishing the cord that connects.

They lead us through doors we may never have opened; down hollow ways we may never have walked; becks we may never have crossed; to countries we may never have visited. They tell of endless possibilities beyond horizons, because, wherever we venture, the heather will flower over Hurst Moor in August and the water that falls over Whitfield Gill Force will search eastwards for the sea.

The dales offer their external magnificence, but also a way into the inner self; humans and place are inextricably entwined. Landscape is both personal and impersonal, external and internal. It shapes our bones, colours our skin, runs through our psyche.

I reclaim the wonder of Gunnerside Gill on a morning in December, lungs edged in frost, each breath relishing the cool decay of the year. Winter in the dales is a time of clarity; nature is stripped back, exposed. There is a wisdom in

---

[176] John Glenday, *Yesnaby*.

winter that no other season possesses. It is elemental. It feels connected. It feels real.

But nature has no care for us. If we look back on halcyon days, we lock ourselves out of reality. Farming has always been a tough existence: grim, heavy, relentless work. For centuries, the plight of the farmer and labourer was forged in unrelenting poverty.

Nature is not about the business of harmony, despite the promotion of the countryside as a social space and a place where sustentation and restoration can be found. The countryside is the result of centuries of man's input, clearing forests, ploughing, re-seeding, draining, enclosing; re-wilding is a continuation of this intervention. But we cannot presume we control the environment, the force that is nature will shape itself.

Unlike humans, nature does not need language to make sense of the world. But it has an internal vocabulary, like the symbiotic relationship between fungi and the roots of trees touching and connecting underground, a network of communication between species which means humans are continually on the back foot.

The old ways of farming may have receded into the past, but the land will outlive today's custodians however we farm, whatever we leave behind. It is tempting to overlook and idolise the lives of those who once worked the land. For most, life was lived hand-to-mouth and we are the poorer if we forget the people that once toiled on small farms. We are their benefactors and so this cycle must continue; future beneficiaries deserve nothing less.

If we touch anywhere after we die, then surely our souls return to the landscapes we haunt when we are alive.

And if fate ee'er compels me to leave this dear spot
In other lands far away roam,
My earnest wish whatee'er be my lot
Is to end my days here at home.[177]

---

[177] Lyrics taken from *Beautiful Dale*, Swaledale anthem. Anon

Acknowledgements

With love and gratitude to Mo for all his encouragement.

To Jane for her support, patience and the hours spent talking about our farming heritage.

The cover image is reproduced with the kind permission of the artist, Helen Alice Johnson. [www.helenalicejohnsonartist.com]

Bibliography

In addition to those works referenced in the footnotes:
- archive.yorkshiredales.org.uk
- *Moral Maze - What is the countryside for?* Michael Buerk, BBC Radio 4, broadcast 23rd February 2022
- Reflections on maps supported by *Maps - Here Be Dragons*, Paul Farley, BBC Radio 4, broadcast 7th April 2019
- Reflections on the wildflower meadows at Muker supported by *Open Country - Hay Meadows*, BBC Radio 4, broadcast 2nd July 2011
- sometimes-interesting.com *Orewinners and Deadmen: Lead Mining in Swaledale*, Guy Carpenter
- swaag.org/GEOLOGY/GeologyIntro.htm, John Russell

www.ingramcontent.com/pod-product-compliance
Lightning Source LLC
Chambersburg PA
CBHW051829160426
43209CB00006B/1099